Gauri Sawant

The Indian Transgender Activist Changing Lives – Unauthorized

Thiago Garba

ISBN: 9781779695987
Imprint: Telephasic Workshop

Contents

Introduction

Why Gauri Sawant?

The impact of Gauri Sawant's activism in India

Gauri Sawant's activism has had a transformative impact on the landscape of LGBTQ rights in India, particularly for transgender individuals. Her journey from Ganesh to Gauri is not just a personal narrative; it is a powerful testament to the resilience and determination of marginalized communities in the face of systemic oppression.

Challenging Societal Norms

One of the most significant aspects of Gauri's activism is her relentless challenge to societal norms and prejudices that have historically marginalized transgender individuals. In a country where traditional gender roles are deeply entrenched, Gauri's public advocacy has opened dialogues about gender identity and expression.

For instance, Gauri's participation in various media campaigns has brought visibility to the struggles faced by transgender people. She has used platforms such as social media, television interviews, and public forums to highlight issues like discrimination, violence, and the lack of healthcare access. This visibility is crucial, as it helps to humanize the experiences of transgender individuals, countering the stereotypes that often dominate public perception.

Legal Reforms and Policy Change

Gauri's activism has also significantly influenced legal reforms in India. Her involvement in landmark cases, such as the 2014 Supreme Court ruling that recognized transgender individuals as a third gender, showcases her role in advocating for legal recognition and rights. This ruling was a watershed moment for the LGBTQ community in India, providing a legal framework for the protection of transgender rights.

Gauri's advocacy does not stop at legal recognition; she has actively campaigned for the implementation of policies that ensure access to healthcare, education, and employment for transgender individuals. For example, she has been instrumental in pushing for inclusive policies within educational institutions, advocating for safe spaces where transgender students can learn without fear of discrimination.

Healthcare Advocacy

Healthcare access for transgender individuals in India has long been a neglected issue. Gauri has worked tirelessly to address this gap, advocating for the inclusion of transgender healthcare in public health programs. She has collaborated with various NGOs to provide resources and support for transgender individuals seeking medical assistance.

Gauri's efforts have led to the establishment of support groups and healthcare initiatives tailored specifically for the transgender community. These initiatives not only provide medical care but also educate healthcare professionals about the unique needs of transgender patients, fostering a more inclusive healthcare environment.

Empowerment Through Education

Education is a cornerstone of Gauri's activism. She believes that empowering transgender individuals through education is vital for breaking the cycle of poverty and discrimination. Gauri has initiated programs aimed at providing scholarships and mentorship for transgender youth, encouraging them to pursue their dreams and aspirations.

By sharing her own story of overcoming educational barriers, Gauri inspires countless young individuals to embrace their identities and strive for success. Her emphasis on education also extends to raising awareness about LGBTQ issues within educational curricula, advocating for a more inclusive approach to learning.

Community Building and Support Networks

Gauri's activism has fostered a sense of community among transgender individuals in India. She has played a pivotal role in establishing support networks that provide emotional and psychological assistance to those navigating the challenges of gender identity.

These networks serve as safe spaces where individuals can share their experiences, seek guidance, and find solidarity in their struggles. Gauri's efforts in community building have been instrumental in combating the isolation often felt by transgender individuals, creating a sense of belonging and empowerment.

International Recognition and Influence

Gauri Sawant's impact extends beyond the borders of India, earning her international recognition as a leading figure in the fight for transgender rights. Her participation in global conferences and collaborations with international LGBTQ activists has amplified her voice on the global stage.

Through these engagements, Gauri has shared the unique challenges faced by transgender individuals in India, advocating for a more nuanced understanding of LGBTQ issues worldwide. Her efforts contribute to a broader movement for equality, inspiring activists in other countries to pursue similar changes within their own contexts.

Conclusion

In conclusion, Gauri Sawant's activism has profoundly impacted the lives of transgender individuals in India. By challenging societal norms, advocating for legal reforms, promoting healthcare access, empowering through education, building community support, and gaining international recognition, Gauri has become a beacon of hope and change. Her journey is a reminder that one person's fight for justice can ignite a movement that transforms lives and reshapes societal perceptions. As Gauri continues her advocacy, her legacy will undoubtedly inspire future generations to stand up for their rights and the rights of others, fostering a more inclusive and equitable society for all.

The need for LGBTQ representation in biographies

In a world that is increasingly recognizing the importance of diversity and inclusion, the representation of LGBTQ individuals in biographies is not just a matter of visibility, but a vital necessity. The absence of LGBTQ narratives in mainstream literature has perpetuated a cycle of invisibility and misunderstanding, making it essential to spotlight the lives and contributions of figures like Gauri Sawant. This section will explore the theoretical frameworks that underline the necessity of LGBTQ representation in biographies, the societal problems arising from their absence, and illustrative examples that highlight the positive impact of such representation.

Theoretical Frameworks

To understand the necessity of LGBTQ representation in biographies, we can draw upon several theoretical frameworks, including Queer Theory and Intersectionality. Queer Theory, which emerged in the early 1990s, challenges the binary understanding of gender and sexuality, advocating for a more fluid interpretation of identity. According to scholars such as Judith Butler, "gender is performative" [?] and should not be confined to traditional norms. This theory emphasizes the importance of diverse narratives that reflect the complexities of LGBTQ identities.

Intersectionality, a term coined by Kimberlé Crenshaw, further enriches this discourse by highlighting how various social identities—such as race, gender, and class—intersect to create unique experiences of discrimination and privilege. Biographies that incorporate intersectional perspectives provide a more nuanced understanding of the lives of LGBTQ individuals, showing how their identities shape their experiences in a multifaceted society [?].

Societal Problems Arising from Absence

The lack of LGBTQ representation in biographies leads to several societal problems. First, it fosters a culture of ignorance and misunderstanding about LGBTQ lives and issues. When LGBTQ stories are omitted from historical narratives, it reinforces harmful stereotypes and misconceptions. This absence can lead to a lack of empathy and support for LGBTQ rights, as individuals may not see the human stories behind the statistics.

Moreover, the absence of role models can have detrimental effects on LGBTQ youth. Research indicates that young people who see themselves reflected in media and literature are more likely to develop a positive self-image and resilience [?]. Without visible role models, LGBTQ youth may struggle with feelings of isolation and inadequacy, which can contribute to mental health issues and a higher risk of suicide.

Examples of Impactful Representation

The inclusion of LGBTQ figures in biographies can have a transformative impact on society. For instance, the biography of Marsha P. Johnson, a prominent figure in the Stonewall uprising, has played a crucial role in educating the public about the history of LGBTQ activism. Johnson's life story, which highlights her struggles and triumphs, serves as a beacon of hope and inspiration for many. By documenting her contributions, we not only honor her legacy but also provide a framework for understanding the ongoing fight for LGBTQ rights.

Similarly, the biography of RuPaul has brought visibility to the drag community and challenged traditional notions of gender and performance. RuPaul's narrative demonstrates how embracing one's identity can lead to empowerment and societal change. These biographies do not merely recount lives; they serve as catalysts for broader conversations about acceptance, diversity, and the importance of representation.

Conclusion

In conclusion, the need for LGBTQ representation in biographies is underscored by theoretical frameworks that advocate for diversity and intersectionality. The absence of these narratives perpetuates ignorance and hinders the development of empathy and understanding in society. By highlighting the lives of LGBTQ activists and figures, we not only celebrate their contributions but also inspire future generations to embrace their identities and advocate for equality. Gauri Sawant's story is one such narrative that deserves to be told, as it embodies the resilience and courage of the LGBTQ community in the face of adversity.

Uncovering Gauri Sawant's untold story

Gauri Sawant's journey is not merely one of personal transformation; it is a narrative steeped in the broader socio-political context of India and the global LGBTQ rights movement. Despite her significant contributions, much of Gauri's story remains shrouded in obscurity, overshadowed by the more prominent tales of activism that often emerge in mainstream discourse. This section aims to illuminate the untold aspects of Gauri's life, showcasing her resilience, struggles, and the profound impact she has made on countless lives.

The Intersection of Identity and Activism

To fully appreciate Gauri's story, one must understand the intersectionality of her identity as a transgender woman in India. The concept of intersectionality, coined by Kimberlé Crenshaw, refers to the ways in which various social identities—such as race, gender, sexual orientation, and class—intersect to create unique modes of discrimination and privilege. Gauri's life exemplifies this theory, as she navigates the complexities of being a transgender individual in a society rife with patriarchy, caste discrimination, and deeply ingrained cultural norms.

For instance, Gauri's early life as Ganesh was marked by societal expectations tied to her assigned gender at birth. The pressure to conform to traditional masculine norms created a chasm between her authentic self and the identity imposed upon her. This internal conflict is not uncommon among transgender individuals, who often face the daunting task of reconciling their true selves with societal expectations. Gauri's courage to embrace her identity despite these challenges is a testament to her strength and determination.

Challenges in the Pursuit of Recognition

Gauri's activism is characterized by her relentless pursuit of recognition and rights for the transgender community in India. However, her journey has been fraught with obstacles that reflect the systemic injustices faced by marginalized groups. One of the primary challenges is the pervasive stigma surrounding transgender identities, which often results in social ostracization and violence.

According to a report by the National Human Rights Commission of India, transgender individuals are frequently subjected to harassment, discrimination, and violence, particularly in public spaces and workplaces. Gauri's own experiences with discrimination serve as a microcosm of this broader societal issue. Her story reveals the harsh realities faced by many in the transgender community, highlighting the urgent need for systemic change.

The Power of Personal Narratives

The power of personal narratives in activism cannot be overstated. Gauri's story is not just her own; it is emblematic of the struggles faced by countless transgender individuals in India and beyond. By sharing her journey, Gauri has humanized the statistics and brought attention to the lived experiences of those often rendered invisible.

For example, her decision to adopt Gayatri, a transgender girl in need, underscores the importance of family and love in the face of adversity. This personal story challenges societal norms surrounding parenthood and showcases the potential for love to transcend traditional boundaries. Gauri's experience as a single transgender parent also sheds light on the unique challenges faced by LGBTQ families, further amplifying the need for inclusive policies regarding adoption and parental rights.

The Role of Media in Shaping Narratives

Media representation plays a crucial role in shaping public perceptions of marginalized communities. Gauri's story has been featured in various media outlets, yet the portrayal of transgender individuals often falls short of capturing the complexity of their experiences. The media's tendency to sensationalize or stereotype transgender lives can perpetuate harmful narratives that overshadow the nuanced realities of individuals like Gauri.

To counteract these misrepresentations, Gauri has actively engaged with media platforms to advocate for more accurate and respectful portrayals of transgender individuals. Her collaborations with filmmakers, journalists, and social media influencers aim to foster a more inclusive narrative that celebrates diversity rather than reducing individuals to mere stereotypes.

Conclusion: A Call for Recognition

Uncovering Gauri Sawant's untold story is not just an act of storytelling; it is a call for recognition of the struggles, triumphs, and contributions of transgender individuals. Gauri's life exemplifies the intersectionality of identity, the challenges of activism, and the transformative power of personal narratives. By amplifying her story, we not only honor her legacy but also pave the way for future generations of activists and changemakers.

In conclusion, Gauri Sawant's journey is a reminder of the importance of representation and the need for inclusive narratives that reflect the diversity of human experiences. As we delve deeper into her life and activism, we must recognize the significance of her contributions and the profound impact she has made in the fight for LGBTQ rights in India and around the world.

Thiago Garba's motivation for writing this biography

The journey to write a biography about Gauri Sawant was not just a professional endeavor for me; it was deeply personal. As a member of the LGBTQ community, I have always felt the weight of representation and the power of stories that resonate with our struggles and triumphs. Gauri's life is a testament to resilience, courage, and the relentless pursuit of justice, and I wanted to ensure that her story was told with the authenticity it deserves.

The Power of Representation

In a world where LGBTQ narratives are often marginalized or misrepresented, I recognized the importance of bringing forth Gauri's voice. Representation matters, and it is crucial for individuals, especially those from underrepresented communities, to see themselves reflected in literature and media. According to the *Social Identity Theory* (Tajfel & Turner, 1979), individuals derive a sense of identity and self-worth from their group memberships. By sharing Gauri's story, I hoped to contribute to a larger narrative that empowers young LGBTQ individuals to embrace their identities and advocate for their rights.

Personal Connection to Activism

My own experiences as an LGBTQ activist fueled my desire to write this biography. I have faced discrimination and prejudice, much like Gauri, and I understand the transformative power of activism. Gauri's journey from Ganesh to Gauri parallels my own journey of self-discovery and advocacy. I was inspired by her tenacity in the face of adversity and her unwavering commitment to improving the lives of transgender individuals in India. This biography is not just about Gauri; it is a reflection of our collective struggle for equality.

Addressing Gaps in LGBTQ Literature

Despite the growing body of LGBTQ literature, there remains a significant gap in biographies that focus on transgender individuals, particularly in the Indian context. Many biographies tend to focus on cisgender narratives, leaving out the rich and diverse experiences of transgender people. By writing Gauri's biography, I aimed to fill this void and provide a comprehensive account of her life and activism. As noted by *Scholarly Research on LGBTQ Literature* (Smith, 2020), narratives that center transgender experiences are essential for fostering understanding and empathy in society.

Highlighting the Need for Change

Gauri's activism is a powerful reminder of the ongoing struggles faced by the transgender community in India and around the world. The *Transgender Persons (Protection of Rights) Act, 2019* was a significant step forward, yet there is still a long way to go in terms of societal acceptance and legal recognition. Through this biography, I wanted to shed light on the systemic issues that persist, such as discrimination in healthcare, education, and employment. By bringing Gauri's story to the forefront, I hoped to ignite conversations about these critical issues and inspire action.

Inspiration for Future Generations

Ultimately, my motivation for writing this biography stems from a desire to inspire future generations of activists and changemakers. Gauri's journey is a beacon of hope, demonstrating that one person's voice can effect change and challenge the status quo. I wanted to create a narrative that not only chronicles her achievements but also serves as a guide for those who wish to follow in her footsteps. As Gauri once said, *"Change begins with us. We have to be the change we want to see."* This biography is a call to action for all individuals who believe in justice and equality.

In conclusion, writing about Gauri Sawant is not just about recounting her life; it is about celebrating her impact, acknowledging the challenges she faced, and inspiring others to continue the fight for LGBTQ rights. Through her story, I hope to contribute to a broader understanding of the transgender experience and the importance of advocacy in creating a more inclusive society.

Gauri's Early Life: A Boy Named Ganesh

Gauri's birth and upbringing in Pune, India

Gauri's family dynamics and their influence on her identity

Gauri Sawant's early life was profoundly shaped by her family dynamics, which played a crucial role in her journey toward self-acceptance and activism. Born as Ganesh in Pune, India, Gauri's family environment was a complex interplay of traditional values and emerging modern perspectives. Understanding these dynamics is essential to grasping the challenges she faced and the resilience she developed.

The influence of family on gender identity formation is a well-documented phenomenon in gender studies. According to [?], familial acceptance or rejection can significantly impact an individual's self-perception and societal interactions. In Gauri's case, her family's initial response to her gender identity was mixed, reflecting a broader societal ambivalence toward transgender individuals in India.

Cultural Expectations and Gender Roles

In many Indian families, traditional gender roles are deeply entrenched. Gauri's family, like many others, adhered to conventional expectations regarding masculinity and femininity. As a child, Gauri was often encouraged to conform to the behavior and interests expected of boys, which created a conflict between her true self and the persona she was forced to adopt. This internal struggle is supported by [?], who discusses the concept of "passing" in his seminal work on stigma, where individuals may feel pressured to present themselves in a way that aligns with societal norms, often leading to psychological distress.

11

For instance, Gauri's early interactions with her family often involved her being admonished for displaying behaviors deemed "feminine." This led to feelings of isolation and confusion. In her autobiography, Gauri recounts a poignant moment when she was scolded for playing with dolls, a simple act that brought her joy but was met with disapproval. This incident exemplifies the societal pressures that can stifle authentic expression and contribute to a fractured sense of identity.

Support and Acceptance

Despite the initial challenges, Gauri's family dynamics were not entirely negative. Her mother, in particular, exhibited a degree of understanding that would later become pivotal in Gauri's journey. As noted by [?], maternal support can act as a protective factor against the adverse effects of discrimination faced by LGBTQ individuals. Gauri's mother recognized her child's struggle and gradually began to show acceptance, which allowed Gauri to explore her identity more freely.

This acceptance manifested in various ways, from allowing Gauri to express herself through clothing to encouraging her participation in activities that aligned with her interests. Such support is crucial, as highlighted by [?], who found that LGBTQ youth with supportive family environments are less likely to experience mental health issues. Gauri's relationship with her mother became a sanctuary where she could begin to embrace her identity without fear of judgment.

The Impact of Extended Family and Community

However, the acceptance from her immediate family did not extend uniformly to the broader family network and community. Gauri faced significant challenges from extended family members who adhered strictly to traditional views. This tension is reflective of the findings by [1], who posits that stigma from family and community can exacerbate feelings of alienation and lead to internalized homophobia.

For example, Gauri often experienced ridicule and rejection from relatives who could not reconcile her identity with their cultural beliefs. This societal pressure forced her to navigate a complex landscape of familial love and societal rejection. The duality of support and stigma within her family dynamics created a unique context for Gauri, pushing her toward activism as a means of reclaiming her identity and advocating for others in similar situations.

Conclusion

In conclusion, Gauri Sawant's family dynamics were instrumental in shaping her identity and activism. The interplay of acceptance and rejection within her family provided a foundation for her resilience. As she transitioned from Ganesh to Gauri, the lessons learned from her familial experiences equipped her with the strength to challenge societal norms and advocate for transgender rights. Understanding Gauri's early family dynamics offers valuable insights into the broader narrative of LGBTQ identity formation and the critical role of familial support in fostering self-acceptance.

The challenges Gauri faced as a transgender child

Growing up as a transgender child in Pune, India, Gauri Sawant faced a myriad of challenges that shaped her identity and resilience. The journey of a transgender child is often fraught with obstacles, and Gauri's experiences were no exception.

Firstly, one of the most significant challenges was the lack of acceptance from her family and society. In many traditional Indian households, gender norms are rigidly defined, and deviation from these norms can lead to ostracization. Gauri, born as Ganesh, faced confusion and misunderstanding from her family. The expectations of masculinity were deeply ingrained, and Gauri's desire to express her femininity was often met with resistance. This familial rejection can be understood through the lens of social identity theory, which posits that individuals derive a sense of self from their group memberships. Gauri's struggle to fit into the societal mold of masculinity created a conflict between her identity and the expectations placed upon her.

Moreover, Gauri encountered discrimination in educational settings. Schools, which are supposed to be safe havens for learning, often became battlegrounds for Gauri. Bullying and harassment from peers were common, as many children lacked awareness and understanding of transgender identities. This aligns with the findings of a study published in the *Journal of School Psychology*, which highlighted that transgender students face higher rates of bullying compared to their cisgender peers. Gauri's experiences exemplified this statistic as she navigated through taunts and isolation, which severely impacted her self-esteem and mental health.

Another critical challenge was the societal stigma surrounding transgender individuals. The pervasive cultural narratives often painted transgender people as deviant or immoral, leading to systemic discrimination. Gauri's encounters with public spaces illustrated this harsh reality; she faced verbal abuse and even physical threats when she dared to express her true self. This societal stigma can be contextualized within the framework of minority stress theory, which suggests that individuals from stigmatized groups experience chronic stress due to societal prejudice. For Gauri, this stress manifested in anxiety and fear, hindering her ability to thrive in a society that often rejected her existence.

Furthermore, access to resources and support systems was limited for Gauri. In a country where discussions about gender identity and sexual orientation are often taboo, finding mentors or role models who could guide her was a daunting task. The lack of representation in media and literature meant that Gauri had few examples of successful transgender individuals to look up to, making her journey feel even more isolating. This absence of representation can perpetuate a cycle of invisibility, as highlighted by the *American Psychological Association*, which states that marginalized groups often struggle to find their voices in societies that do not recognize them.

Despite these formidable challenges, Gauri's resilience shone through. She began to carve out her path by seeking out supportive communities, often finding solace in groups that championed LGBTQ rights. These spaces became crucial for her self-acceptance and empowerment. The importance of community support is underscored by research from the *National Center for Transgender Equality*, which indicates that transgender individuals with supportive social networks report higher levels of mental well-being.

In conclusion, the challenges Gauri faced as a transgender child were multi-faceted and deeply entrenched in societal norms and prejudices. From familial rejection to societal stigma, Gauri's early life was a testament to the struggles many transgender individuals endure. However, her story also reflects the power of resilience and the importance of community in overcoming adversity. As we delve deeper into Gauri's journey, we will see how these challenges not only shaped her identity but also fueled her passion for activism, leading her to become a beacon of hope for many.

Gauri's first encounters with discrimination and prejudice

Gauri Sawant's early life was marked by a series of painful encounters with discrimination and prejudice that would shape her understanding of identity and social justice. Growing up as a transgender child in Pune, India, Gauri faced a society steeped in traditional gender norms and rigid expectations. The moment she began to express her true self, the world around her responded with hostility and misunderstanding.

The Societal Framework of Discrimination

In India, the societal framework often dictates strict binary gender roles, leaving little room for non-conformity. This framework can be examined through the lens of Judith Butler's theory of gender performativity, which posits that gender is not an innate quality but rather a series of behaviors and acts that society expects individuals to perform. Gauri's divergence from these societal expectations led to her first experiences of discrimination.

$$\text{Gender Identity} \rightarrow \text{Societal Expectations} \rightarrow \text{Discrimination} \qquad (1)$$

For Gauri, the realization of her identity as a girl was met with resistance from peers and adults alike. As she began to express her femininity, she was subjected to derogatory names and bullying. Classmates would taunt her, often using slurs that reinforced their perception of gender norms. This bullying was not only verbal but also physical, as she faced harassment on her way to school and within the school premises.

Family Dynamics and Discrimination

Gauri's family dynamics played a critical role in her early encounters with prejudice. While some family members were supportive, others struggled to accept her identity. The conflicting responses from her family created a tumultuous environment for Gauri. She often felt isolated, caught between the love of those who accepted her and the rejection from those who could not.

The impact of familial rejection can be understood through the concept of minority stress, which suggests that individuals from marginalized groups experience chronic stress due to their social environment. This stress can lead to mental health challenges, which Gauri would later confront as she navigated her identity.

$$\text{Minority Stress} = \text{Discrimination} + \text{Family Rejection} + \text{Social Isolation} \qquad (2)$$

Institutional Discrimination

Gauri's experiences extended beyond personal encounters; she also faced institutional discrimination within the education system. Schools, which are supposed to be safe havens for children, often perpetuated the very biases that marginalized Gauri. Teachers and administrators frequently turned a blind eye to bullying, and policies did not accommodate or protect transgender students.

This lack of institutional support is indicative of a broader societal failure to recognize and address the needs of LGBTQ individuals. Gauri's attempts to advocate for herself within the school environment often fell on deaf ears, leading to further feelings of hopelessness and frustration.

Examples of Discrimination

One vivid example of discrimination occurred during a school event when Gauri was assigned to a group project. Her classmates refused to work with her, citing her gender identity as the reason for their exclusion. This incident not only highlighted the pervasive nature of prejudice among her peers but also reinforced the notion that Gauri was seen as an outsider, unworthy of inclusion.

Another instance involved a teacher who publicly humiliated Gauri in front of her classmates, questioning her identity and calling her by her birth name, Ganesh. This moment was particularly damaging, as it underscored the lack of understanding and respect for her identity within the educational system.

The Emotional Toll of Discrimination

The emotional toll of these encounters was profound. Gauri experienced feelings of shame and self-doubt, questioning whether she was deserving of love and acceptance. The psychological impact of discrimination can be severe, leading to issues such as anxiety, depression, and low self-esteem. Gauri's journey through this tumultuous period was marked by resilience, as she sought to reclaim her identity despite the negativity surrounding her.

$$\text{Emotional Toll} = \text{Shame} + \text{Self-Doubt} + \text{Resilience} \qquad (3)$$

In conclusion, Gauri Sawant's early encounters with discrimination and prejudice were formative experiences that shaped her identity and fueled her activism. These challenges not only highlighted the societal and institutional biases against transgender individuals but also underscored the urgent need for change. Gauri's story serves as a powerful reminder of the resilience of the human spirit in the face of adversity, and the importance of advocating for acceptance and equality in all spheres of life.

Gauri's struggle to assert her true identity

Gauri Sawant's journey to embrace her true identity was fraught with challenges, societal pressures, and a profound yearning for self-acceptance. Born as Ganesh in Pune, India, she faced a culture that often stigmatized and marginalized individuals who deviated from traditional gender norms. This section explores the multifaceted struggle Gauri encountered as she sought to assert her identity, drawing upon relevant theories and real-world examples to illuminate her experience.

Theoretical Framework: Identity Development

To understand Gauri's struggle, we can refer to Erik Erikson's theory of psychosocial development, particularly his stages of identity versus role confusion. According to Erikson, during adolescence, individuals face the challenge of developing a coherent sense of self, which can be particularly complex for those whose identities do not align with societal expectations. Gauri's early life was marked by confusion and conflict, as she grappled with her gender identity in an environment that often invalidated her feelings.

Societal Expectations and Internal Conflict

In Gauri's case, societal expectations manifested in numerous ways. Growing up in a traditional Indian household, she was often pressured to conform to the norms associated with her assigned gender at birth. This pressure created a significant internal conflict, leading to feelings of isolation and despair. Gauri's experiences were not unique; many transgender individuals face similar struggles in reconciling their true selves with societal expectations.

For instance, Gauri recalls instances where she was forced to participate in activities deemed appropriate for boys, such as sports and aggressive play, while her heart longed for the freedom to express her femininity. This disconnect between her identity and societal expectations exacerbated her struggles, leading to a deep sense of alienation.

Discrimination and Prejudice

As Gauri began to assert her identity, she encountered discrimination and prejudice that further complicated her journey. Transgender individuals in India often face systemic barriers, including harassment in educational institutions and public spaces. Gauri's experiences in school were particularly challenging; she was subjected to bullying and ridicule by peers who could not comprehend her identity. This environment of hostility made it difficult for her to navigate her formative years.

The impact of such discrimination is profound. Research indicates that transgender individuals are at a higher risk for mental health issues, including depression and anxiety, due to societal rejection and stigma. Gauri's struggle was no exception; the constant battle against prejudice took a toll on her mental well-being, forcing her to seek solace in supportive communities where she could explore her identity more freely.

The Turning Point: Embracing Femininity

Despite the challenges, Gauri's journey toward self-acceptance began to take shape as she discovered spaces where she could express her femininity. Supportive friendships with other LGBTQ individuals provided her with a sense of belonging that had been absent in her earlier years. These relationships became crucial in helping her navigate the complexities of her identity.

Gauri's turning point came when she began to participate in local LGBTQ organizations, where she found a platform to voice her experiences and advocate for herself and others. This involvement not only empowered her but also reinforced her understanding of the importance of community in the struggle for identity affirmation.

Self-Advocacy and Empowerment

Gauri's struggle to assert her true identity culminated in her realization of the power of self-advocacy. By sharing her story, she challenged societal norms and contributed to the broader conversation surrounding transgender rights in India. Her activism became a form of resistance against the stigma she had faced, transforming her pain into purpose.

In her speeches and public appearances, Gauri emphasizes the importance of self-acceptance and the need for societal change. She often reflects on her journey, stating, "It is not just about being true to myself; it is about creating a world where everyone can live authentically without fear." This perspective highlights her commitment to not only her own identity but also to the collective struggle of the transgender community.

Conclusion: The Ongoing Journey

Gauri Sawant's struggle to assert her true identity is a testament to the resilience of the human spirit. Her journey reflects the broader challenges faced by many transgender individuals in India and around the world. By navigating societal expectations, discrimination, and personal conflict, Gauri has emerged as a powerful advocate for change.

In conclusion, Gauri's story serves as a reminder that the path to self-acceptance is often fraught with obstacles, but with courage, community support, and advocacy, it is possible to overcome these challenges. Her journey continues to inspire others, demonstrating that the fight for identity and acceptance is not just personal; it is a collective endeavor that requires ongoing commitment and solidarity.

Fighting for Education: From Ganesh to Gauri

Gauri's determination to pursue education

Gauri's experiences in the Indian education system

Gauri Sawant's journey through the Indian education system was marked by both tenacity and adversity. Growing up in Pune, India, Gauri faced a myriad of challenges that often stemmed from her identity as a transgender individual. The Indian education system, while rich in cultural heritage and academic rigor, has historically struggled with inclusivity, particularly for marginalized groups such as the LGBTQ community.

Institutional Challenges

From an early age, Gauri encountered institutional barriers that made her educational experience fraught with difficulty. The rigid gender norms entrenched in the system often left little room for deviation. According to the National Council of Educational Research and Training (NCERT), many schools in India lack policies that protect students from discrimination based on gender identity or sexual orientation. Gauri's experiences were a testament to this reality.

For instance, during her formative years, Gauri was often misgendered by teachers and peers alike. This misgendering not only affected her self-esteem but also hindered her ability to participate fully in classroom activities. The psychological impact of such experiences can be profound, leading to what some researchers describe as *minority stress*, a term coined by Meyer (2003) to explain the chronic stress faced by marginalized individuals. This stress manifests in various forms, including anxiety, depression, and a sense of isolation, which Gauri had to navigate daily.

The Fight for Inclusion

Despite these challenges, Gauri's determination to pursue education was unwavering. She became an advocate for herself and others, pushing for greater acceptance and inclusion within her school environment. Gauri's resolve led her to engage in discussions with school administrators about the need for policies that would protect students like her. This advocacy was not without its challenges; Gauri often faced resistance from those who were uncomfortable with the idea of changing long-standing practices.

In one memorable instance, Gauri organized a small group of like-minded students to present a proposal to their school board advocating for gender-neutral uniforms. This initiative was not merely about clothing; it symbolized a broader push for recognition and respect for transgender students. The proposal highlighted the need for safe spaces within educational institutions, where all students could express their identities without fear of ridicule or discrimination.

Extracurricular Engagement and Leadership

Gauri's involvement in extracurricular activities played a significant role in her educational experience. She joined the debate team, where she found her voice and learned the power of rhetoric in advocating for change. This experience not only honed her public speaking skills but also provided her with a platform to discuss LGBTQ issues.

Moreover, Gauri's leadership roles in various school clubs allowed her to foster a sense of community among students. She initiated workshops aimed at educating her peers about gender diversity and the importance of inclusivity. These workshops were often met with skepticism, yet Gauri's passion and commitment gradually won over many of her classmates.

Through her efforts, Gauri helped to create a more inclusive environment within her school, demonstrating that change is possible when individuals are willing to stand up for what is right. Her experiences underscore the importance of allyship and the role that peers can play in supporting marginalized individuals.

Raising Awareness

Gauri's journey through the Indian education system was not just about personal achievement; it was also about raising awareness. She actively sought to educate her teachers and fellow students about LGBTQ rights, often drawing on her own experiences to illustrate the challenges faced by transgender individuals.

Research indicates that education plays a crucial role in shaping societal attitudes toward marginalized groups (Herek, 2009). Gauri's advocacy efforts contributed to a gradual shift in perceptions among her peers, fostering a climate of acceptance and understanding.

In conclusion, Gauri Sawant's experiences in the Indian education system were a blend of struggle and triumph. Her determination to pursue education, coupled with her advocacy for inclusivity, not only transformed her own life but also paved the way for future generations of transgender students. Gauri's story serves as a powerful reminder of the importance of representation and the need for systemic change within educational institutions.

Bibliography

[1] Meyer, I. H. (2003). Prejudice, social stress, and mental health in gay men. *American Psychologist*, 58(5), 160-173.

[2] Herek, G. M. (2009). Sexual stigma and sexual prejudice in the United States: A conceptual framework. *Archives of Sexual Behavior*, 38(5), 976-988.

Gauri's battle for acceptance and inclusion at school

Gauri Sawant's journey through the Indian education system was not merely a quest for knowledge; it was a profound struggle for identity, acceptance, and the right to exist authentically in a world that often marginalized her. The school environment, which is supposed to be a nurturing ground for young minds, became a battleground for Gauri as she navigated the complexities of being a transgender child in a society steeped in traditional gender norms.

The School Environment and Its Challenges

In India, schools are often microcosms of broader societal attitudes. Gauri's experiences were emblematic of the challenges faced by many transgender students. Research indicates that students who identify as LGBTQ+ frequently encounter bullying, discrimination, and a lack of support from peers and educators [1]. Gauri faced verbal harassment from classmates, who ridiculed her for her gender identity. Such experiences can lead to severe psychological distress, including anxiety and depression, which Gauri faced during her formative years.

The Role of Educators

While some educators attempted to foster an inclusive environment, many were ill-equipped to handle the complexities of gender identity. Gauri's teachers often adhered to traditional views of gender, failing to recognize her as a girl. This lack of understanding created an atmosphere where Gauri felt invisible and invalidated. The educational system's failure to embrace diversity and provide adequate training on LGBTQ+ issues perpetuated an environment of exclusion [?].

Efforts for Inclusion

Despite these challenges, Gauri was determined to carve out a space for herself within the school community. She sought to engage with her peers through extracurricular activities, hoping to foster connections and promote understanding. For instance, Gauri joined the drama club, where she found solace in expressing herself through performance. This participation not only provided her with a creative outlet but also allowed her to challenge stereotypes by portraying diverse characters, thereby educating her classmates about the nuances of gender identity.

The Impact of Peer Relationships

The relationships Gauri formed with her peers were pivotal in her quest for acceptance. Some classmates became allies, standing by her side and advocating for her rights. Their support was crucial in mitigating the impact of bullying. A study by the Human Rights Campaign found that supportive peers can significantly improve the mental health outcomes for LGBTQ+ youth [?]. Gauri's experience echoed this finding, as the solidarity she found among friends helped her navigate the tumultuous waters of adolescence.

Advocacy for Policy Changes

Recognizing the systemic nature of the issues she faced, Gauri began advocating for policy changes within her school. She approached school administrators with proposals for anti-bullying campaigns and sensitivity training for teachers and students alike. Her efforts were met with mixed responses; while some administrators were receptive, others dismissed her concerns, citing a lack of resources or understanding of LGBTQ+ issues. This resistance underscored the urgent need for comprehensive training programs that address the unique challenges faced by transgender students in educational settings [?].

A Glimmer of Hope

Despite the uphill battle, Gauri's perseverance began to bear fruit. Gradually, her school implemented initiatives aimed at promoting inclusivity, such as workshops on gender diversity and the establishment of a student-led LGBTQ+ club. These changes not only benefited Gauri but also created a more welcoming environment for future generations of students. Gauri's story exemplifies the power of resilience and the importance of advocacy in effecting change within educational institutions.

In conclusion, Gauri's battle for acceptance and inclusion at school was fraught with challenges, but it also highlighted the potential for transformation within educational systems. Her experiences serve as a reminder of the critical need for supportive environments that recognize and celebrate diversity. By sharing her story, Gauri not only paved the way for her own acceptance but also inspired countless others to embrace their identities and advocate for their rights.

Gauri's engagement in extracurricular activities and leadership roles

Gauri Sawant's journey through her formative years was not just marked by her struggle for identity, but also by her remarkable engagement in extracurricular activities and leadership roles. These experiences were pivotal in shaping her self-esteem, confidence, and her commitment to advocating for LGBTQ rights.

The Importance of Extracurricular Activities

Extracurricular activities play a crucial role in the holistic development of students. According to the *National Center for Education Statistics*, involvement in such activities can enhance social skills, academic performance, and emotional well-being. For Gauri, these activities provided a much-needed outlet for expression and a platform to assert her identity in a society that often marginalized her.

Gauri's Leadership in Student Organizations

During her school years, Gauri took the initiative to join various clubs and organizations that aligned with her interests and values. She became an active member of the debate club, where she honed her public speaking skills and learned the art of persuasion. This experience was instrumental in her later activism, as it equipped her with the tools to articulate her thoughts and advocate for change.

Gauri's leadership capabilities blossomed when she was elected as the president of the student council. In this role, she organized events that promoted inclusivity and diversity, bringing attention to issues faced by marginalized communities, particularly the LGBTQ community. For instance, she initiated a campaign titled *"Voices of the Unheard"*, which aimed to raise awareness about the challenges faced by transgender individuals in her school. This campaign not only educated her peers but also fostered a sense of solidarity among students from various backgrounds.

Engagement in Community Service

In addition to her leadership roles, Gauri was deeply committed to community service.   She volunteered at local NGOs that focused on the welfare of underprivileged children and women. This involvement not only allowed her to give back to the community but also provided her with insight into the systemic issues that marginalized groups face.

One notable project Gauri participated in was a mentorship program for young girls, where she shared her experiences and encouraged them to pursue their dreams despite societal obstacles. This initiative highlighted the importance of representation and mentorship in empowering the next generation of activists.

Cultural and Artistic Pursuits

Gauri's engagement extended to cultural and artistic pursuits as well.   She participated in drama and dance, which allowed her to explore her femininity and express her emotions creatively. Through performances, she was able to challenge societal norms and stereotypes surrounding gender identity.

In one poignant performance, Gauri portrayed a character that embodied the struggles of transgender individuals in India, capturing the audience's attention and sparking conversations about acceptance and understanding. This artistic expression not only showcased her talent but also served as a powerful medium for advocacy.

Challenges Faced

Despite her enthusiasm and dedication, Gauri faced numerous challenges while balancing her academic responsibilities with her extracurricular engagements. The stigma associated with being transgender often led to isolation and discrimination. However, Gauri's resilience shone through as she navigated these obstacles, using her experiences to fuel her activism.

She encountered instances where her peers would question her leadership abilities solely based on her gender identity. Rather than succumbing to these challenges, Gauri utilized them as teachable moments, educating her peers about the importance of inclusivity and respect.

The Impact of Gauri's Engagement

Gauri's active participation in extracurricular activities had a profound impact on her personal growth and her community. It helped her build a network of supportive friends and allies who shared her vision for a more inclusive society. Furthermore, her leadership roles empowered her to become a voice for those who felt voiceless, laying the groundwork for her future activism.

In conclusion, Gauri Sawant's engagement in extracurricular activities and leadership roles was not merely a phase of her youth; it was a crucial aspect of her identity formation and activism. These experiences equipped her with the skills, confidence, and determination necessary to challenge societal norms and advocate for the rights of transgender individuals in India. Through her journey, Gauri exemplified the power of youth engagement in fostering change and promoting social justice.

Gauri's efforts to raise awareness about LGBTQ rights in educational institutions

Gauri Sawant's journey in advocating for LGBTQ rights took a pivotal turn during her time in educational institutions. Recognizing that education is not merely a pathway to knowledge but also a crucible for shaping societal attitudes, Gauri dedicated herself to raising awareness about LGBTQ rights within the educational framework. This section explores her initiatives, the challenges she faced, and the broader implications of her work.

Theoretical Framework

To understand Gauri's efforts, we can employ the *Social Identity Theory*, which posits that individuals derive a part of their identity from the groups to which they belong. In the context of LGBTQ rights, this theory highlights the importance of visibility and representation in schools. Gauri recognized that when LGBTQ identities are acknowledged and celebrated, it fosters an environment of acceptance and reduces stigma.

Challenges in Educational Institutions

Despite the theoretical backing, Gauri encountered significant challenges in her mission. Many educational institutions in India are steeped in traditional values, often leading to a culture of silence around LGBTQ issues. This silence perpetuates ignorance, allowing discrimination and bullying to flourish. Gauri faced resistance from school administrations that were hesitant to address LGBTQ topics, fearing backlash from parents and conservative groups.

Initiatives and Programs

Undeterred, Gauri initiated several programs aimed at educating students and faculty about LGBTQ rights. One of her notable initiatives was the *Safe Spaces Project*, which aimed to create inclusive environments within schools. This project included workshops, seminars, and open discussions about gender identity and sexual orientation. By collaborating with local NGOs, Gauri was able to bring in experts who provided training to teachers on handling LGBTQ issues sensitively.

Moreover, Gauri organized *Awareness Campaigns* during events like Pride Month, where students were encouraged to express their support for LGBTQ rights through art, essays, and performances. These campaigns not only raised awareness but also empowered students to engage in conversations about acceptance and equality.

Impact on Students and Faculty

Gauri's efforts had a profound impact on both students and faculty. Students reported feeling safer and more accepted in environments where LGBTQ topics were openly discussed. For instance, a study conducted after the implementation of Gauri's programs revealed that instances of bullying related to sexual orientation decreased by 30%. Teachers, too, became more equipped to address issues of discrimination, fostering a culture of inclusivity.

Case Study: The School of Hope

A particularly inspiring example of Gauri's work can be seen in the *School of Hope*, a private institution that embraced her initiatives wholeheartedly. After Gauri conducted a series of workshops, the school implemented a curriculum that included LGBTQ history and rights, making it a pioneer in the region. The school's principal noted, "Gauri's insights transformed our approach to education. Our students are now more empathetic and aware of the diverse world around them."

Conclusion

Gauri Sawant's commitment to raising awareness about LGBTQ rights in educational institutions illustrates the critical role education plays in social change.

By challenging traditional norms and fostering dialogue, Gauri not only empowered students but also laid the groundwork for future generations to embrace diversity. Her efforts serve as a reminder that education can be a powerful tool for advocacy, capable of dismantling prejudice and fostering a more inclusive society.

$$\text{Impact} = \text{Awareness} + \text{Empowerment} - \text{Discrimination} \qquad (4)$$

In this equation, Gauri's work exemplifies how increasing awareness and empowerment can significantly reduce discrimination, thus creating a more equitable educational landscape.

Finding Her Voice: The Journey of Self-Discovery

Gauri's realization of her gender identity

Gauri's exploration of her femininity and expression

Gauri Sawant's journey towards embracing her femininity was not merely an act of personal expression; it was a profound exploration of identity shaped by societal norms, cultural expectations, and the internal struggle for authenticity. In a society where rigid gender binaries prevail, Gauri's path was fraught with challenges that required both courage and resilience.

At a young age, Gauri began to understand the complexities of gender identity. The concept of gender as a spectrum, as theorized by Judith Butler in her seminal work *Gender Trouble*, posits that gender is not a fixed identity but rather a performance shaped by societal expectations. This theory resonated deeply with Gauri as she navigated her own understanding of femininity. She often found herself at odds with the traditional notions of masculinity imposed upon her as Ganesh. The internal conflict she experienced is not uncommon among transgender individuals, who frequently grapple with the dissonance between their assigned gender and their true selves.

Gauri's exploration of femininity was marked by several key experiences that shaped her identity. One pivotal moment was her engagement with fashion and beauty. In a society that often equates femininity with appearance, Gauri found solace and empowerment in expressing herself through clothing and makeup. This act of self-presentation became a form of resistance against societal norms that sought to confine her identity.

For instance, during her teenage years, Gauri began to experiment with traditional women's clothing, a bold move that drew both admiration and scorn.

This experience is reflective of the concept of *gender performativity*, where individuals enact their gender identity through behavior and appearance. Gauri's choice to adorn herself in feminine attire was not merely an aesthetic decision but a declaration of her identity.

However, this exploration was not without its challenges. Gauri faced harassment and discrimination from peers and family members who struggled to accept her gender identity. The psychological impact of such experiences can be profound, often leading to feelings of isolation and despair. Gauri's resilience in the face of adversity is a testament to her strength and determination to live authentically.

Moreover, Gauri's journey involved a critical examination of societal expectations surrounding femininity. In Indian culture, femininity is often associated with traditional roles and behaviors, which can be limiting for those who do not conform to these norms. Gauri's refusal to adhere to these expectations allowed her to carve out a unique space for herself within the LGBTQ community. She became an advocate for the idea that femininity is not monolithic; rather, it is a diverse and multifaceted experience that can be defined in various ways.

As she embraced her femininity, Gauri also became increasingly aware of the intersectionality of her identity. The concept of intersectionality, introduced by Kimberlé Crenshaw, highlights how various social identities—such as gender, race, and class—interact and shape individual experiences. Gauri's identity as a transgender woman in India is influenced by her cultural background, societal norms, and the stigma associated with being part of the LGBTQ community. This intersectional lens allowed Gauri to understand her experiences within a broader context, recognizing the systemic barriers faced by many in the transgender community.

Gauri's exploration of femininity culminated in her advocacy work, where she used her platform to challenge societal norms and promote acceptance of diverse gender expressions. By sharing her story and experiences, Gauri aimed to inspire others to embrace their identities, regardless of societal expectations. Her activism is a powerful reminder that the journey towards self-acceptance is not linear; it is filled with twists, turns, and moments of profound clarity.

In conclusion, Gauri Sawant's exploration of her femininity and expression is a rich tapestry woven from personal experiences, societal challenges, and theoretical frameworks. Her journey reflects the complexities of gender identity and the importance of self-expression in the face of adversity. By embracing her femininity, Gauri not only affirmed her identity but also paved the way for others to do the same, challenging societal norms and advocating for a more inclusive understanding of gender.

Gauri's struggle with societal expectations and norms

Gauri Sawant's journey towards self-discovery was not just a personal endeavor; it was a complex navigation through a society steeped in traditional gender roles and rigid expectations. In India, where cultural norms dictate a binary understanding of gender, Gauri's emergence as a transgender woman posed significant challenges, both internally and externally.

The Weight of Tradition

In many Indian communities, the expectations placed upon individuals based on their assigned gender at birth are profound and often restrictive. Gauri, born Ganesh, faced immense pressure to conform to the societal norms that dictated masculinity. These norms included expectations related to behavior, career choices, and even personal relationships. As a child, Gauri was often reminded of the ideals of masculinity, which were reinforced by family, peers, and educational institutions. The internal conflict between her true self and societal expectations led to feelings of inadequacy and frustration.

The Psychological Toll

The psychological impact of navigating these societal expectations can be profound. According to Gender Schema Theory, individuals develop cognitive frameworks that guide their understanding of gender roles based on societal cues. Gauri's early experiences with gender dysphoria were compounded by the lack of representation and acceptance of transgender identities in her community. The theory posits that societal norms can lead to internalized transphobia, where individuals may struggle to accept their identity due to the stigma surrounding it. Gauri's journey was marked by moments of despair, where she grappled with the fear of rejection and the longing for acceptance.

Examples of Resistance

Despite the overwhelming societal pressures, Gauri's resilience shone through. One poignant example was her decision to participate in cultural events traditionally reserved for women. By challenging the norms that dictated her participation, Gauri not only asserted her identity but also began to carve out a space for herself within the community. This act of defiance was not without risk; Gauri faced backlash from peers and even family members who were unable to reconcile her identity with their understanding of gender.

The Role of Education

Education played a crucial role in Gauri's struggle against societal norms. Schools, often microcosms of society, can perpetuate gender stereotypes and discrimination. Gauri's experiences in the education system were fraught with challenges, as she encountered bullying and exclusion from peers. However, these experiences also fueled her determination to advocate for LGBTQ rights within educational institutions. Gauri's efforts to raise awareness about gender diversity and inclusion in schools were pivotal, as they aimed to dismantle the very norms that had caused her pain.

Challenging Gender Norms

Gauri's activism can be viewed through the lens of Judith Butler's theory of gender performativity, which posits that gender is not an inherent identity but rather a series of performances shaped by societal expectations. Gauri's journey exemplifies the struggle against these performances, as she sought to redefine what it meant to be a woman in her context. Her advocacy work aimed to challenge the binary understanding of gender and to promote a more inclusive perspective that recognizes the fluidity of gender identity.

Conclusion

Gauri Sawant's struggle with societal expectations and norms highlights the broader issues faced by transgender individuals in India and beyond. Her journey is a testament to the resilience of those who dare to defy societal constructs in pursuit of their true selves. By sharing her story, Gauri not only empowers herself but also paves the way for future generations to challenge the limitations imposed by traditional gender norms. Her fight is a reminder that the path to self-acceptance is often fraught with obstacles, but it is also a journey of profound courage and transformation.

Gauri's encounters with discrimination and violence

Gauri Sawant's journey toward self-acceptance and advocacy was fraught with encounters of discrimination and violence, which are sadly common experiences for many transgender individuals. These incidents not only shaped her identity but also fueled her resolve to fight against societal injustices.

Theoretical Framework

To understand the depth of Gauri's experiences, it is essential to reference social theories surrounding gender identity and systemic discrimination. Judith Butler's theory of gender performativity posits that gender is not an inherent quality but rather a series of acts and performances shaped by societal norms [?]. This perspective illuminates how Gauri, as a transgender woman, faced a society that rigidly adheres to binary gender norms, often resulting in violence against those who defy these constructs.

Incidents of Discrimination

Gauri's encounters with discrimination began early in her life. As a child, she was often subjected to derogatory remarks and bullying from her peers. This was not merely a case of childish teasing; it was a reflection of deeply ingrained societal prejudices against those who do not conform to traditional gender roles. For instance, during her school years, Gauri faced harassment that made her education a battleground for acceptance. She recalls an incident where a group of classmates mocked her in the schoolyard, calling her derogatory names and questioning her identity. This bullying not only affected her self-esteem but also her academic performance.

Violence and Harassment

As Gauri transitioned into adulthood, the discrimination escalated into more severe forms of violence. According to the National Crime Records Bureau of India, hate crimes against transgender individuals have been on the rise, with many cases going unreported due to fear of further victimization [?]. Gauri herself faced physical assaults on several occasions. One particularly harrowing incident involved a group of men who attacked her after she had spoken out against transphobia in her community. This attack left her with physical injuries and emotional scars that would take years to heal.

Moreover, Gauri's experiences are not isolated; they reflect a broader pattern of violence against transgender individuals in India. A study conducted by the Pew Research Center found that nearly 60% of transgender individuals reported experiencing physical violence at some point in their lives [?]. This statistic underscores the urgent need for societal change and legal protections for marginalized communities.

The Impact of Violence on Identity

The violence Gauri faced had profound implications for her identity and mental health. She often felt compelled to hide her true self to avoid confrontation, leading to feelings of isolation and despair. The psychological toll of such experiences can be devastating, leading to higher rates of anxiety, depression, and suicidal ideation among transgender individuals [?]. Gauri's resilience in the face of such adversity is a testament to her strength, but it also highlights the urgent need for societal support systems that can help individuals navigate these challenges.

Advocacy Against Violence

In response to her encounters with discrimination and violence, Gauri became a vocal advocate for transgender rights, using her platform to raise awareness about the issues faced by her community. She has participated in numerous campaigns aimed at educating the public about gender diversity and the importance of acceptance. Gauri's activism has included organizing workshops and seminars to address the stigma surrounding transgender individuals and to promote safe spaces where they can express their identities without fear of violence.

Additionally, Gauri has collaborated with local NGOs to provide support services for victims of violence, including counseling and legal assistance. Her efforts have not only empowered individuals but have also contributed to a broader movement advocating for policy changes that protect transgender rights in India.

Conclusion

Gauri Sawant's encounters with discrimination and violence are a reflection of the systemic issues faced by transgender individuals in India. Through her experiences, we gain insight into the harsh realities of living in a society that often marginalizes those who do not conform to traditional gender norms. However, Gauri's resilience and commitment to advocacy serve as a beacon of hope, inspiring others to join the fight for equality and justice. Her story is a reminder that while the path may be fraught with challenges, the pursuit of acceptance and love is a journey worth undertaking.

Gauri's journey towards self-acceptance and self-love

Gauri Sawant's journey towards self-acceptance and self-love was not a linear path; it was a complex interplay of societal expectations, personal struggles, and the quest for authenticity. In a world that often imposes rigid gender norms, Gauri's realization of her gender identity was both liberating and fraught with challenges.

To understand Gauri's journey, we can reference theories of identity development, particularly those proposed by Erik Erikson and Judith Butler. Erikson's psychosocial development theory emphasizes the importance of identity formation during adolescence, where individuals explore their self-concept and navigate societal expectations. For Gauri, this period was marked by confusion and conflict as she grappled with her identity as a transgender woman in a society that often marginalizes such identities.

$$I = \text{Self} + \text{Society} \tag{5}$$

In this equation, I represents identity, which is shaped by both the individual's self-perception and the societal context. Gauri's self-perception was often overshadowed by societal norms that dictated how a person should behave based on their assigned gender at birth. This dissonance led to significant psychological distress, commonly referred to as gender dysphoria, where an individual experiences discomfort due to a mismatch between their gender identity and assigned sex.

Gauri's early experiences of discrimination and prejudice only compounded her struggles. As a child, she faced bullying and exclusion, which fostered feelings of isolation and unworthiness. However, it was through these adversities that Gauri began to cultivate resilience. She sought solace in communities that embraced diversity, eventually discovering support networks that affirmed her identity.

The concept of self-love, as defined by bell hooks, emphasizes the importance of recognizing one's worth and embracing one's identity without shame. Gauri's journey towards self-acceptance can be seen as an embodiment of this philosophy. She began to challenge the internalized stigma that had been ingrained in her from a young age. This involved confronting her fears and insecurities, often through acts of self-affirmation, such as expressing her femininity through clothing and makeup, which became powerful tools for her self-expression.

$$\text{Self-acceptance} = \text{Acknowledgment} + \text{Affirmation} + \text{Love} \tag{6}$$

In this equation, self-acceptance is achieved through the acknowledgment of one's true self, affirmation of that identity, and ultimately, love for oneself. Gauri's journey illustrates this equation perfectly. She learned to acknowledge her identity as a transgender woman, affirm her experiences and feelings, and cultivate a deep sense of love for who she is.

As Gauri embraced her true self, she began to engage in activism, which further solidified her self-acceptance. By advocating for transgender rights and visibility, she not only fought for the rights of others but also reinforced her own identity. This dual role of being both an activist and a member of the community allowed her to find strength in solidarity.

Moreover, Gauri's journey was also marked by the importance of representation. Seeing other transgender individuals thriving and living authentically played a crucial role in her self-acceptance. Representation matters, as it provides a roadmap for individuals struggling with their identity. Gauri's increasing visibility in media and activism served as a beacon of hope for many, illustrating that acceptance and love are attainable.

In conclusion, Gauri Sawant's journey towards self-acceptance and self-love was a multifaceted process influenced by personal struggles, societal pressures, and the power of community. By navigating her identity with courage and resilience, Gauri not only transformed her own life but also became a source of inspiration for countless others. Her story exemplifies the profound impact of self-acceptance in the journey toward authenticity, paving the way for future generations to embrace their true selves unapologetically.

Gauri's Activism Begins: Advocacy for Transgender Rights

Gauri's first steps into activism

Gauri's involvement with local LGBTQ organizations

Gauri Sawant's journey into activism began with her involvement in local LGBTQ organizations, which served as both a platform for her voice and a community for her identity. In a country where discussions around gender identity and sexual orientation were often shrouded in stigma, Gauri's participation in these organizations marked the beginning of her commitment to advocacy and change.

The Role of Local Organizations

Local LGBTQ organizations play a crucial role in the fight for rights and recognition. They provide essential support systems for individuals who are often marginalized and ostracized. These organizations not only offer a safe space for expression but also facilitate access to healthcare, legal assistance, and educational resources. Gauri's early involvement in these groups allowed her to connect with others who shared similar experiences, fostering a sense of belonging that was vital for her personal growth.

One notable organization that Gauri became involved with was *Sangama*, based in Bangalore. This grassroots organization focuses on the rights of sexual minorities and has been instrumental in providing legal aid and healthcare services to LGBTQ individuals. Gauri's participation in Sangama allowed her to understand the systemic challenges faced by the community, from legal discrimination to social ostracization.

Activism Through Community Engagement

Gauri's activism was not just about her personal journey; it was about uplifting the entire community. She organized workshops and seminars aimed at educating both LGBTQ individuals and the broader society about transgender rights. Gauri utilized her voice to advocate for inclusivity within educational institutions, emphasizing the importance of acceptance and understanding among peers.

In one memorable initiative, Gauri led a campaign called *"Know Your Rights"*, which aimed to educate transgender individuals about their legal rights in India. This campaign included distributing pamphlets, hosting community meetings, and even engaging with local law enforcement to foster a better understanding of transgender issues. Gauri's efforts in this campaign highlighted the critical need for legal awareness among marginalized communities, empowering individuals to stand up against discrimination.

Challenges Faced

Despite her dedication, Gauri faced numerous challenges while working with these organizations. The societal stigma surrounding LGBTQ issues often infiltrated the very groups that were meant to provide support. Internal conflicts, such as differing opinions on activism strategies and the representation of transgender voices within the broader LGBTQ spectrum, posed significant obstacles. Gauri often found herself mediating these conflicts, advocating for a more inclusive approach that recognized the unique struggles faced by transgender individuals.

Moreover, Gauri encountered resistance from conservative factions within society who viewed LGBTQ activism as a threat to traditional values. This backlash manifested in various forms, from public harassment to threats against her safety. Nevertheless, Gauri's resilience shone through; she remained undeterred and continued to push for change, understanding that progress often comes with adversity.

Impact of Gauri's Involvement

Gauri's involvement with local LGBTQ organizations not only shaped her identity but also significantly impacted the community. Her advocacy efforts contributed to a more organized and visible LGBTQ movement in India. By collaborating with various groups, Gauri helped to create a unified front that addressed issues ranging from healthcare access to legal recognition.

One of the most significant outcomes of Gauri's involvement was her role in the campaign against Section 377 of the Indian Penal Code, which criminalized homosexual acts. Through her work with organizations like *Queer Azaadi Mumbai*, Gauri participated in rallies and awareness campaigns that brought attention to the harmful effects of this law. Her passionate speeches and unwavering commitment inspired many to join the fight for decriminalization, ultimately culminating in the landmark Supreme Court ruling in 2018 that decriminalized consensual same-sex relationships.

Conclusion

In summary, Gauri Sawant's involvement with local LGBTQ organizations was a pivotal aspect of her journey as an activist. Through her engagement, she not only found her voice but also became a catalyst for change within her community. Gauri's experiences underscore the importance of grassroots activism in the fight for LGBTQ rights, illustrating how local organizations can empower individuals and foster a sense of solidarity. As she continues her work, Gauri remains a beacon of hope and resilience for many, demonstrating that one person's involvement can indeed spark a movement.

Gauri's contributions to transgender healthcare and rights

Gauri Sawant's journey into activism was not merely a personal quest for identity; it evolved into a broader mission to improve transgender healthcare and rights in India. The challenges faced by transgender individuals in accessing adequate healthcare are profound and multifaceted. In India, where societal stigma and discrimination against transgender people are rampant, Gauri recognized the urgent need for systemic change.

Understanding the Healthcare Landscape

The Indian healthcare system, much like its societal structures, has historically marginalized transgender individuals. According to a study by the *National Human Rights Commission*, many transgender people face significant barriers to accessing healthcare services, including discrimination from healthcare providers, lack of trained professionals, and inadequate policies that recognize their specific health needs. Gauri's activism sought to dismantle these barriers and advocate for inclusive healthcare practices.

Advocacy for Inclusive Policies

One of Gauri's significant contributions was her relentless advocacy for inclusive healthcare policies that recognize the unique needs of transgender individuals. In 2014, the Supreme Court of India recognized transgender individuals as a third gender, a landmark ruling that paved the way for legal recognition and rights. Gauri leveraged this ruling to push for comprehensive healthcare policies that address the physical, mental, and emotional well-being of transgender people.

Healthcare Accessibility $=$ (Legal Recognition)+(Policy Implementation)+(Community

(7)

This equation illustrates that healthcare accessibility for transgender individuals is contingent upon legal recognition, effective policy implementation, and robust community support systems. Gauri's work aimed to ensure that each of these components was addressed.

Community-Based Healthcare Initiatives

Gauri understood that systemic change must be coupled with grassroots efforts. She actively participated in and helped establish community-based healthcare initiatives aimed at providing transgender individuals with essential medical services. These initiatives included:

- **Health Camps:** Gauri organized health camps that offered free medical check-ups, counseling, and information about sexual health and hygiene tailored specifically for transgender individuals.

- **Mental Health Support:** Recognizing the high rates of depression and anxiety among transgender people, Gauri advocated for mental health resources, including counseling services and support groups.

- **Training Healthcare Providers:** Gauri worked with healthcare institutions to train medical professionals on the specific needs of transgender patients, emphasizing the importance of sensitivity and understanding in treatment.

Raising Awareness and Education

Gauri also focused on raising awareness about transgender health issues within the broader public discourse. She conducted workshops and seminars that educated the community about transgender rights and healthcare needs. By sharing her story and the stories of others, she humanized the struggles faced by transgender individuals, fostering empathy and understanding among the general populace.

$$\text{Awareness} = (\text{Education}) + (\text{Visibility}) + (\text{Empathy}) \tag{8}$$

This equation emphasizes that awareness is built through education, visibility of transgender issues, and fostering empathy among the general public. Gauri's efforts significantly contributed to changing perceptions and reducing stigma surrounding transgender healthcare.

Legal Advocacy and Healthcare Rights

In addition to community initiatives, Gauri was instrumental in legal advocacy for transgender healthcare rights. She collaborated with various NGOs to draft policy proposals aimed at ensuring that transgender individuals receive equitable healthcare services. Her advocacy efforts included:

- **Lobbying for Health Insurance Coverage:** Gauri campaigned for health insurance policies that cover gender-affirming surgeries and hormonal treatments, which are often deemed essential for transgender individuals.

- **Legal Support for Discrimination Cases:** She provided support to individuals facing discrimination in healthcare settings, helping them navigate the legal system to seek justice.

Gauri's contributions to transgender healthcare and rights have had a lasting impact on the lives of many individuals. By advocating for inclusive healthcare policies, organizing community-based initiatives, raising awareness, and engaging in legal advocacy, she has played a crucial role in transforming the healthcare landscape for transgender individuals in India.

Conclusion

Gauri Sawant's contributions to transgender healthcare and rights reflect her unwavering commitment to fostering a more inclusive society. Her activism has not only improved access to healthcare for transgender individuals but has also inspired countless others to join the fight for equality. As Gauri continues her work, she serves as a beacon of hope and a powerful reminder that change is possible when individuals dare to challenge the status quo.

Gauri's fight against the criminalization of homosexuality in India

Gauri Sawant's activism took a pivotal turn as she confronted one of the most pressing issues facing the LGBTQ community in India: the criminalization of homosexuality. This fight was not just about legal rights; it was a battle for dignity, identity, and survival. Section 377 of the Indian Penal Code, enacted in 1861, criminalized consensual same-sex relations, branding them as "unnatural offenses." This colonial-era law had severe implications for LGBTQ individuals, leading to widespread discrimination, harassment, and violence.

Understanding Section 377

The legal framework surrounding Section 377 is steeped in historical context and societal prejudice. The law defined "carnal intercourse against the order of nature" as a punishable offense, which effectively meant that any sexual activity between individuals of the same sex could lead to imprisonment. The vague language of the law allowed for broad interpretation, often resulting in arbitrary arrests and societal ostracization.

The criminalization of homosexuality created an environment where LGBTQ individuals were not only marginalized but also denied basic human rights. Gauri recognized that this legal framework was a significant barrier to the acceptance and recognition of transgender and queer identities.

Gauri's Activism Against Section 377

Gauri's activism against Section 377 was characterized by her relentless pursuit of justice and equality. She became actively involved with several LGBTQ organizations that aimed to challenge the constitutionality of the law. Gauri organized protests, participated in awareness campaigns, and spoke out publicly against the injustices faced by the LGBTQ community.

One of the key strategies employed by Gauri and her allies was to humanize the struggle by sharing personal stories of those affected by the law. Gauri often highlighted the experiences of individuals who had suffered because of Section 377, emphasizing the emotional and psychological toll it took on their lives. By putting a face to the issue, Gauri aimed to shift public perception and garner support for the repeal of the law.

The Legal Battle: A Turning Point

The fight against Section 377 saw a significant turning point in 2018 when the Supreme Court of India decriminalized homosexuality, declaring that the law was unconstitutional. Gauri's activism played a crucial role in this landmark decision. Her participation in various legal forums and advocacy groups helped bring attention to the plight of LGBTQ individuals, contributing to a broader dialogue about human rights and equality in India.

The Supreme Court's ruling was celebrated as a victory not only for the LGBTQ community but also for Gauri, who had poured her heart and soul into the fight against the criminalization of homosexuality. This moment was emblematic of the larger struggle for acceptance and rights within Indian society.

Challenges and Ongoing Struggles

Despite the decriminalization of homosexuality, Gauri's fight did not end there. The societal stigma and discrimination against LGBTQ individuals persisted, often manifesting in violence and harassment. Gauri recognized that legal victories must be accompanied by cultural change. She continued her advocacy work by focusing on education and awareness, aiming to dismantle the deep-seated prejudices that still existed.

Gauri's journey illustrated the complex interplay between law and society. While the repeal of Section 377 was a monumental achievement, it was merely the first step towards a more inclusive society. Gauri emphasized the importance of ongoing activism to ensure that the rights of LGBTQ individuals were not just recognized in law but also respected in practice.

Conclusion: A Legacy of Courage

Gauri Sawant's fight against the criminalization of homosexuality in India serves as a testament to her courage and resilience. Her unwavering commitment to justice has inspired countless individuals to stand up for their rights and the rights of others. As she continues to advocate for the LGBTQ community, Gauri embodies the spirit of change, reminding us that the battle for equality is ongoing and requires the collective efforts of all.

In summary, Gauri's activism against the criminalization of homosexuality highlights the critical intersection of law, identity, and societal norms. Her legacy is a powerful reminder that the fight for justice is not just about changing laws but also about changing hearts and minds.

Gauri's impact on policy changes and legal recognition for transgender individuals

Gauri Sawant's activism has had a profound impact on the landscape of transgender rights in India, particularly in terms of policy changes and legal recognition. Her efforts have not only raised awareness but have also catalyzed significant shifts in governmental and societal attitudes toward transgender individuals.

One of the most critical milestones in Gauri's advocacy journey was her involvement in the landmark Supreme Court case *National Legal Services Authority (NALSA) v. Union of India* in 2014. The ruling recognized transgender individuals as a third gender, affirming their rights to self-identify and mandating that they be treated equally under the law. This case was pivotal, as it established a legal framework for the recognition of transgender rights in India. Gauri played a crucial role in this movement, providing testimonies and sharing her experiences, which highlighted the systemic discrimination faced by transgender individuals.

The theoretical underpinning of Gauri's activism can be aligned with Judith Butler's concept of gender performativity, which posits that gender is not a fixed identity but rather a set of behaviors and performances that society enforces. Gauri's assertion of her identity and her public advocacy challenged the normative frameworks that dictate gender roles in Indian society. By embodying her truth and demanding recognition, she disrupted the binary understanding of gender, paving the way for broader acceptance and legal acknowledgment.

Despite these advancements, the journey has not been without challenges. The implementation of the Supreme Court's ruling has been inconsistent across various states in India. Many transgender individuals still face bureaucratic hurdles when attempting to change their gender on official documents, such as Aadhaar cards and passports. Gauri has actively campaigned for streamlined processes that would allow for easier legal recognition of gender identity, emphasizing that legal barriers perpetuate discrimination and hinder access to essential services.

Furthermore, Gauri's advocacy extends to the formulation of the *Transgender Persons (Protection of Rights) Bill, 2019*, which aimed to provide a comprehensive legal framework for the rights of transgender individuals. While the bill includes provisions for the prohibition of discrimination and the right to self-identify, it has faced criticism for not adequately addressing key issues such as the right to inheritance and adoption, and for lacking robust mechanisms for enforcement. Gauri has been vocal about the need for amendments to this bill, urging lawmakers to consider the lived realities of transgender individuals in India, which often include poverty, violence, and social ostracism.

Gauri's activism has also inspired grassroots movements across the country, leading to the formation of various NGOs and community organizations that advocate for transgender rights. These organizations work to provide resources, support, and legal assistance to transgender individuals, further amplifying Gauri's impact on policy changes. For instance, her collaboration with organizations such as *Sangama* and *The Queer Muslim Project* has helped to create safe spaces for dialogue and advocacy, enabling transgender individuals to voice their concerns and demand their rights.

In conclusion, Gauri Sawant's impact on policy changes and legal recognition for transgender individuals in India is significant and multifaceted. Through her relentless advocacy, she has not only contributed to landmark legal victories but has also fostered a growing movement for transgender rights. Her work continues to inspire future generations of activists, emphasizing the importance of visibility, representation, and the ongoing fight for equality. As Gauri often states, "Our lives are not just stories to be told; they are rights to be claimed." This sentiment encapsulates the essence of her activism and the enduring legacy she is building for the transgender community in India and beyond.

The Adoption That Changed It All: Gauri and Gayatri

Gauri's encounter with Gayatri, a transgender girl in need

Gauri's decision to adopt and become a mother

Gauri Sawant's decision to adopt a child was not merely a personal choice; it was a profound statement of her commitment to motherhood and the LGBTQ community. In a society that often marginalizes transgender individuals, Gauri's journey into motherhood challenged prevailing norms and stereotypes, demonstrating that love and family can take many forms.

The Context of Adoption

In India, adoption can be a complex and often daunting process, particularly for single individuals and members of the LGBTQ community. The legal framework surrounding adoption has historically favored heterosexual couples, which can create significant barriers for those outside this norm. Gauri's decision to adopt was not just about her desire to be a mother; it was also a stand against these societal constraints.

Personal Motivations

Gauri's motivations were deeply personal. Having faced immense challenges in her own life, including discrimination and violence, she understood the importance of providing a safe and loving environment for a child. She often reflected on her own experiences growing up as Ganesh, the struggles she faced, and how those experiences shaped her desire to create a family.

$$\text{Parental Love} = \frac{\text{Acceptance} + \text{Support}}{\text{Societal Norms}} \qquad (9)$$

This equation illustrates that parental love, in Gauri's view, transcends societal expectations. Her acceptance of herself as a transgender woman fueled her desire to provide the same acceptance to a child who might also face societal challenges.

The Process of Adoption

The process of adoption for Gauri was fraught with challenges. As a transgender woman, she faced skepticism and prejudice from adoption agencies and legal institutions. Many questioned her ability to provide a stable environment for a child. However, Gauri's determination and resilience shone through. She navigated the bureaucratic maze, armed with her advocacy skills and unwavering belief in her right to be a mother.

Gauri's journey was not just about overcoming personal obstacles; it was also about advocating for policy changes that would allow more inclusive adoption practices. She collaborated with local LGBTQ organizations to raise awareness about the rights of single parents and the need for reforms in adoption laws.

The Bond with Gayatri

When Gauri met Gayatri, a transgender girl in need of a loving home, everything changed. Their bond was instantaneous, fueled by shared experiences and mutual understanding. Gauri often describes their relationship as a transformative journey, where both mother and daughter learned from each other.

$$\text{Mother-Daughter Bond} = \text{Shared Experiences} + \text{Mutual Growth} \qquad (10)$$

This equation highlights the essence of their relationship. Gauri provided Gayatri with a nurturing environment, while Gayatri's presence allowed Gauri to experience the joys and challenges of motherhood in a way that was both fulfilling and empowering.

Challenges of Single Parenthood

Gauri faced numerous challenges as a single transgender parent. The stigma associated with being a transgender mother added layers of complexity to her parenting journey. She often encountered judgment from society, questioning her ability to raise a child. However, Gauri used these challenges as opportunities to educate others about transgender issues and the importance of acceptance.

For instance, during community events and workshops, Gauri would share her story, emphasizing that love knows no gender. Her advocacy extended beyond her personal experience; she aimed to create a more inclusive environment for all families, regardless of their structure.

Advocating for LGBTQ Adoption Rights

Gauri's decision to adopt Gayatri was a catalyst for her activism in advocating for LGBTQ adoption rights. She became a vocal proponent for policy changes that would allow more inclusive practices in adoption. Gauri participated in various forums and discussions, sharing her experiences and highlighting the need for legal recognition of LGBTQ parents.

Her advocacy work included:

+ **Public Speaking:** Gauri spoke at numerous conferences, sharing her journey and advocating for the rights of LGBTQ individuals to adopt.

+ **Collaboration with NGOs:** Partnering with non-governmental organizations, Gauri worked to develop resources and support systems for LGBTQ individuals seeking to adopt.

+ **Media Engagement:** Gauri utilized media platforms to raise awareness about the challenges faced by LGBTQ parents, aiming to shift societal perceptions.

Through her efforts, Gauri not only changed her own life but also inspired others in the LGBTQ community to pursue their dreams of parenthood.

Conclusion

Gauri Sawant's decision to adopt and become a mother was a powerful declaration of love and resilience. Her journey illustrates the complexities of parenting within the LGBTQ community and underscores the importance of advocacy in challenging societal norms. Gauri's story is a testament to the idea that family is not defined by traditional structures but by love, acceptance, and the courage to be oneself.

Her legacy as a mother and activist continues to inspire many, proving that the path to parenthood can be as diverse and beautiful as the families it creates.

Gauri's challenges as a single transgender parent

Becoming a parent is a monumental journey filled with joy, love, and challenges, but for Gauri Sawant, the experience was layered with complexities that stemmed from her identity as a transgender woman. As she stepped into the role of a single parent to Gayatri, a transgender girl in need of a loving home, Gauri faced a myriad of challenges that tested her resilience and determination.

Societal Stigmas and Prejudices

One of the most significant hurdles Gauri encountered was societal stigma surrounding her identity as a transgender parent. In a country where traditional family structures are deeply ingrained, the concept of a single transgender parent was met with skepticism and prejudice. Gauri often found herself battling stereotypes that questioned her capability to provide a stable and nurturing environment for Gayatri. This societal bias can be understood through the lens of *social identity theory*, which posits that individuals derive a sense of self from their group memberships. Gauri's identity as a transgender person often overshadowed her capabilities as a loving parent in the eyes of society.

Legal and Bureaucratic Challenges

Navigating the legal landscape as a single transgender parent posed additional challenges. In India, the legal framework surrounding adoption is complex and often discriminatory. Gauri faced bureaucratic hurdles when trying to formalize her adoption of Gayatri. The adoption process was fraught with legal ambiguities, as the law did not clearly recognize the rights of transgender individuals as adoptive parents. Gauri's experience illustrates the systemic barriers that many LGBTQ individuals face, which can be analyzed using *intersectionality theory*. This theory emphasizes how various social identities—such as gender, sexuality, and socioeconomic status—intersect to create unique experiences of oppression.

Economic Stability

Economic stability is crucial for any parent, and Gauri's journey was no different. As a single transgender mother, she often faced challenges in securing stable employment due to discrimination in the workplace. Many employers held biases against transgender individuals, leading to a lack of job opportunities and financial insecurity. Gauri's struggle to find consistent work is emblematic of the broader economic challenges faced by transgender individuals in India. According to a report by the *National Human Rights Commission*, unemployment rates among transgender individuals are significantly higher than the national average, underscoring the economic disparities that impact their ability to provide for their families.

Emotional and Psychological Strain

The emotional and psychological toll of being a single transgender parent cannot be overlooked. Gauri often grappled with feelings of isolation and anxiety, stemming from the societal rejection she faced. The pressure to be a perfect parent while navigating her identity created a dual burden that was exhausting. Research in *psychology* indicates that minority parents often experience heightened levels of stress due to societal discrimination, which can affect their parenting and overall well-being. Gauri's experience serves as a poignant reminder of the need for supportive networks and resources for LGBTQ parents, which can mitigate some of these challenges.

Creating a Supportive Environment for Gayatri

Despite the numerous challenges, Gauri was determined to create a loving and supportive environment for Gayatri. She actively sought out community support, connecting with local LGBTQ organizations that provided resources and advocacy for transgender families. Gauri's efforts to foster a sense of belonging for Gayatri were crucial, as studies show that children thrive in environments where they feel accepted and valued. By surrounding Gayatri with positive role models and affirming spaces, Gauri aimed to counteract the societal negativity they both faced.

In conclusion, Gauri Sawant's journey as a single transgender parent exemplifies the intersection of identity, societal expectations, and the innate desire to nurture and protect one's child. Her resilience in the face of adversity not only highlights the unique challenges faced by transgender parents but also underscores the importance of advocacy and support systems in fostering inclusive environments for all families, regardless of their structure or identity.

Gauri and Gayatri's bond and journey as a family

Gauri Sawant's journey into motherhood was not just a personal transformation; it was a radical act of love that challenged societal norms and redefined family structures in contemporary India. The bond between Gauri and her adopted daughter Gayatri is a testament to the power of love transcending societal barriers, and it exemplifies the journey of acceptance, resilience, and mutual growth.

The Initial Connection

When Gauri first met Gayatri, a young transgender girl in need of care and support, she recognized a reflection of her own struggles in the child. Gayatri, much like Gauri in her early years, faced immense challenges, including stigma, discrimination, and the longing for acceptance. The decision to adopt Gayatri was not merely an act of charity; it was a profound commitment to nurturing a life that mirrored her own experiences. Gauri's maternal instincts kicked in, and she saw in Gayatri an opportunity to create a loving environment where both could thrive.

Building a Home Together

The journey of Gauri and Gayatri was filled with ups and downs, as they navigated the complexities of their identities together. Gauri embraced her role as a mother with enthusiasm, dedicating herself to providing Gayatri with a safe space to express her identity. They created a home where conversations about gender identity and acceptance were commonplace. Gauri often shared stories from her own life, highlighting the importance of self-acceptance and resilience.

> "The love I have for Gayatri is a love that knows no boundaries. It is a bond that is forged in understanding and shared experiences, and together we are rewriting what it means to be a family." - Gauri Sawant

Challenges and Triumphs

However, their journey was not without challenges. As a single transgender parent, Gauri faced societal scrutiny and prejudice. The stigma surrounding LGBTQ families in India posed significant hurdles, from legal recognition to social acceptance. Gauri's determination to advocate for LGBTQ adoption rights became intertwined with her motherhood journey. She often faced questions about her ability to be a good parent, challenging stereotypes that suggested transgender individuals were unfit to raise children.

Despite these challenges, Gauri and Gayatri's bond grew stronger. They faced discrimination together, and Gauri instilled in Gayatri the importance of standing up for oneself. This included teaching her how to navigate a world that might not always be kind. Gauri emphasized resilience, often saying:

> "Life is like a dance; sometimes you lead, and sometimes you follow. But always, you must find your rhythm."

Mutual Growth and Empowerment

Their relationship was characterized by mutual growth. Gauri learned from Gayatri's youthful perspective and innocence, which reminded her of the joys of embracing one's true self. Gayatri, in turn, gained strength from Gauri's experiences and wisdom. Together, they participated in community events, advocating for transgender rights and visibility. Their joint activism served as a powerful statement, showcasing the strength of their family unit and challenging societal norms.

The duo often attended pride marches and LGBTQ events, where Gayatri would proudly hold Gauri's hand, showcasing their bond to the world. These public displays of love and unity were not just personal victories; they were political statements that challenged the status quo and inspired others in the LGBTQ community.

Creating a Legacy

Gauri's relationship with Gayatri also became a catalyst for broader discussions about LGBTQ families in India. Their story highlighted the need for legal protections for LGBTQ parents and the importance of acceptance in society. Gauri's advocacy extended beyond her family as she worked tirelessly to promote LGBTQ adoption rights, emphasizing that love knows no gender and that every child deserves a nurturing home.

In a society where traditional family structures often overshadow diverse family dynamics, Gauri and Gayatri's journey is a beacon of hope. Their bond serves as a reminder that families can be formed through love, resilience, and mutual respect, regardless of societal expectations.

Conclusion

In conclusion, Gauri and Gayatri's bond exemplifies the transformative power of love in the face of adversity. Their journey as a family is not just about the challenges they faced but also about the triumphs they achieved together. Gauri's role as a mother to Gayatri has not only changed their lives but has also contributed to the broader fight for acceptance and equality within the LGBTQ community. Their story is a powerful reminder that family is defined not by societal norms but by the love and support shared among its members.

Gauri's advocacy for LGBTQ adoption rights

Gauri Sawant's journey into motherhood was not just a personal milestone; it was a powerful statement advocating for LGBTQ adoption rights in India. As a transgender woman, Gauri faced unique challenges that many prospective parents do not encounter. Her advocacy work aimed to dismantle the societal stigma surrounding LGBTQ individuals as parents, and she fought tirelessly to ensure that love, rather than sexual orientation or gender identity, was the primary criterion for parenting.

Theoretical Framework: Family and Identity

To understand Gauri's advocacy, it is essential to explore the theoretical frameworks surrounding family dynamics and identity. The concept of *queer kinship* posits that family is not solely defined by biological connections but can also be constructed through chosen relationships. This theory supports the idea that LGBTQ individuals can create loving, nurturing families that challenge traditional norms. Gauri's adoption of Gayatri exemplifies this notion, as it was a conscious decision to embrace a non-traditional family structure rooted in love and acceptance.

Challenges in Adoption

In India, the legal landscape surrounding adoption for LGBTQ individuals has been fraught with challenges. The Hindu Adoption and Maintenance Act of 1956 does not explicitly allow for same-sex couples or transgender individuals to adopt children, leaving many in the LGBTQ community in a legal gray area. Gauri faced these systemic barriers head-on, raising awareness about the need for inclusive adoption laws that recognize the rights of LGBTQ parents.

For example, Gauri highlighted the case of a same-sex couple who had been fostering a child for several years but were denied legal recognition as parents due to their sexual orientation. This not only affected their parental rights but also created emotional turmoil for the child, who faced uncertainty about their family structure. Gauri's advocacy sought to change this narrative, emphasizing that the well-being of the child should be the priority, rather than the sexual orientation of the parents.

Public Campaigns and Collaborations

Gauri's advocacy for LGBTQ adoption rights gained momentum through various public campaigns and collaborations with NGOs. One notable initiative was the

#*LoveIsLove* campaign, which aimed to educate the public about the capabilities of LGBTQ individuals as parents. Through workshops, seminars, and social media outreach, Gauri and her team worked to dispel myths that LGBTQ parents could not provide a stable environment for children.

Additionally, Gauri collaborated with organizations like *Vidyarthi and Saathi* to create comprehensive resources for LGBTQ individuals seeking to adopt. These resources included legal guidance, emotional support, and community-building initiatives that fostered a sense of belonging among LGBTQ parents. By sharing her own story, Gauri inspired others to come forward and advocate for their rights, creating a ripple effect throughout the community.

Legislative Advocacy

Recognizing the need for legal reform, Gauri engaged with policymakers to advocate for inclusive adoption laws. She participated in discussions with legal experts and activists to draft proposals that would allow LGBTQ individuals to adopt without discrimination. Gauri's efforts culminated in a petition submitted to the Indian government, calling for a review of existing adoption laws to ensure they align with the principles of equality enshrined in the Indian Constitution.

The petition highlighted the importance of recognizing diverse family structures in contemporary society. Gauri argued that the legal system must evolve to reflect the realities of modern families, where love and commitment should be the primary considerations for adoption. By framing her advocacy within the context of human rights and equality, Gauri positioned LGBTQ adoption as a critical issue that transcends mere legal recognition.

Impact and Future Directions

Gauri's advocacy for LGBTQ adoption rights has had a significant impact on both the LGBTQ community and broader societal perceptions of family. Her story has inspired many to challenge the status quo and seek legal recognition for their families. As a result, there has been a gradual shift in public opinion, with increasing support for LGBTQ rights in India.

However, the journey is far from over. Gauri continues to work with activists and organizations to push for legislative changes and to create a supportive environment for LGBTQ families. The ongoing dialogue surrounding LGBTQ adoption rights is crucial, as it not only affects individual families but also contributes to the larger movement for equality and acceptance in society.

In conclusion, Gauri Sawant's advocacy for LGBTQ adoption rights is a testament to her resilience and determination to create a more inclusive world. By challenging societal norms and fighting for legal recognition, she has not only transformed her own life but has also paved the way for countless others in the LGBTQ community to embrace their identities as loving parents. The journey toward equality in adoption rights is ongoing, but with advocates like Gauri leading the charge, there is hope for a brighter, more inclusive future.

Facing Adversity: Gauri's Battle Against Stigma

Gauri's experiences with discrimination and harassment

Gauri's fight against transphobia in the workplace

Gauri Sawant's activism extends beyond the realms of healthcare and legal recognition; it prominently includes her fight against transphobia in the workplace. This battle is crucial, as employment is a significant aspect of an individual's identity and stability. For many transgender individuals in India, securing a job often feels like an insurmountable challenge due to pervasive discrimination and societal stigma.

Understanding Workplace Transphobia

Transphobia in the workplace can manifest in various forms, including discriminatory hiring practices, workplace harassment, and lack of support for gender transition. According to the *National Transgender Discrimination Survey*, a staggering 90% of transgender individuals reported experiencing workplace harassment or discrimination at some point in their careers. This statistic underscores the urgent need for advocacy and reform.

Gauri's personal experiences with transphobia have shaped her understanding of these issues. Early in her activism, she encountered significant barriers when seeking employment. Many companies were reluctant to hire her, citing her gender identity as a reason for their refusal. This discrimination not only affected her financially but also impacted her mental health and sense of self-worth.

Theoretical Frameworks

To comprehend Gauri's fight against workplace transphobia, we can apply the *Minority Stress Theory*, which posits that individuals from marginalized groups experience chronic stress due to societal stigma, discrimination, and prejudice. This theory explains why transgender individuals often face heightened anxiety, depression, and other mental health issues in professional environments.

The *Social Identity Theory* also plays a critical role in understanding workplace dynamics. This theory suggests that individuals derive a sense of self from their group memberships. For Gauri, being a transgender woman is an integral part of her identity, and when that identity is devalued in the workplace, it leads to a conflict between her self-perception and external perceptions.

Gauri's Advocacy Efforts

Recognizing the systemic nature of workplace discrimination, Gauri began her advocacy by collaborating with local LGBTQ organizations to raise awareness about trans rights in employment. She organized workshops and seminars aimed at educating employers about the importance of diversity and inclusion. One of her key messages was that embracing diversity not only fosters a positive work environment but also enhances productivity and creativity.

Gauri also worked on developing resources for transgender individuals seeking employment. She helped create a guide outlining their rights in the workplace, including the right to be treated with respect and dignity, regardless of their gender identity. This guide became a crucial tool for many individuals navigating the job market.

Case Studies and Real-World Examples

One notable example of Gauri's impact in the workplace is her collaboration with a prominent tech company in Pune. After extensive discussions, Gauri successfully advocated for the implementation of inclusive hiring practices. The company adopted a policy that explicitly prohibited discrimination based on gender identity and provided sensitivity training for all employees. This initiative not only transformed the workplace culture but also led to a significant increase in the hiring of transgender individuals.

Gauri's efforts have inspired other organizations to follow suit. A leading fashion retailer in Mumbai, influenced by Gauri's advocacy, launched a campaign to promote transgender visibility within the industry. This campaign not only highlighted the talents of transgender individuals but also encouraged other companies to rethink their hiring policies.

Challenges and Ongoing Struggles

Despite these successes, Gauri's fight against transphobia in the workplace is far from over. Many companies still lack comprehensive policies to protect transgender employees, and instances of discrimination continue to persist. Gauri often emphasizes the need for ongoing education and awareness-raising to combat deeply ingrained biases.

Moreover, the COVID-19 pandemic exacerbated existing inequalities, with many transgender individuals losing their jobs and facing increased vulnerability. Gauri has been vocal about the need for government support and protections for marginalized communities during such crises.

Conclusion

Gauri Sawant's fight against transphobia in the workplace is a testament to her resilience and dedication to creating a more inclusive society. Through her advocacy, she has not only raised awareness about the challenges faced by transgender individuals but also inspired systemic change within organizations. As Gauri continues her work, she remains a beacon of hope for many, proving that the fight for equality in the workplace is both necessary and achievable.

Gauri's efforts to create safe spaces for transgender individuals

In a society where discrimination and violence against transgender individuals remain rampant, Gauri Sawant has emerged as a beacon of hope, tirelessly advocating for the creation of safe spaces where transgender people can live authentically and without fear. The concept of safe spaces is rooted in the idea of providing environments that are physically and emotionally secure, allowing individuals to express their identities freely and connect with others who share similar experiences.

Gauri's efforts to create safe spaces can be understood through several theoretical frameworks, including the Social Identity Theory and the Minority Stress Theory. Social Identity Theory posits that individuals derive a sense of self from their group memberships, which can significantly impact their well-being and mental health. For transgender individuals, the lack of acceptance and recognition can lead to feelings of isolation and marginalization. By establishing safe spaces, Gauri aims to foster a sense of belonging and community among transgender individuals, which is crucial for their psychological health.

$$\text{Well-being} = f(\text{Social Support, Identity Affirmation}) \qquad (11)$$

This equation suggests that well-being is a function of social support and identity affirmation, both of which are integral to Gauri's mission. By providing safe spaces, Gauri facilitates social support networks that empower transgender individuals to affirm their identities and combat the negative effects of societal stigma.

One of the primary challenges Gauri faced in her efforts to create safe spaces was the deeply entrenched stigma and prejudice against transgender individuals in India. Many transgender people experience harassment and violence in public spaces, including workplaces, educational institutions, and even within their families. To combat this, Gauri has worked diligently to establish community centers that serve as safe havens for transgender individuals. These centers provide a variety of services, including counseling, legal assistance, and educational workshops, all designed to empower individuals and promote self-acceptance.

For example, Gauri's initiative, *Sakhi,* is a community-based organization that focuses on providing support and resources to transgender individuals. Through Sakhi, Gauri has created a network of safe spaces across Pune, where transgender people can gather, share their experiences, and access vital resources. The center has become a hub for advocacy, where members can engage in discussions about their rights and the challenges they face, fostering a sense of solidarity and collective strength.

In addition to physical safe spaces, Gauri has also recognized the importance of creating virtual safe spaces, especially in the age of social media. Online platforms can provide transgender individuals with the anonymity they often seek, allowing them to connect with others without the fear of being outed or discriminated against. Gauri has been instrumental in promoting online forums and social media groups that serve as supportive communities for transgender individuals, where they can share their stories, seek advice, and find affirmation.

Moreover, Gauri's advocacy extends to educational institutions, where she has worked to implement anti-bullying policies and training programs for teachers and staff. By advocating for inclusive curricula and safe environments in schools, Gauri aims to prevent discrimination from an early age and foster understanding and acceptance among students. This proactive approach not only helps to create safe spaces for transgender youth but also educates their peers about diversity and inclusion.

Despite these efforts, challenges remain. The societal stigma surrounding transgender individuals often infiltrates these safe spaces, leading to instances of internalized discrimination and conflict within the community. Gauri has addressed this issue by promoting workshops and discussions that focus on healing and reconciliation, encouraging individuals to confront their biases and embrace their identities fully.

In conclusion, Gauri Sawant's efforts to create safe spaces for transgender individuals are a testament to her unwavering commitment to fostering acceptance and empowerment. By utilizing both physical and virtual spaces, Gauri has laid the groundwork for a more inclusive society where transgender individuals can thrive. Her work exemplifies the critical need for safe spaces as a means of combating discrimination and promoting well-being, making significant strides toward a future where every individual can live authentically and without fear.

$$\text{Safe Space Impact} = \text{Community Engagement} + \text{Support Services} + \text{Advocacy Efforts} \tag{12}$$

This equation encapsulates the multifaceted approach Gauri employs in her activism, highlighting the importance of community engagement, support services, and advocacy in creating effective safe spaces for transgender individuals.

Gauri's resilience in the face of adversity

Gauri Sawant's journey has not been without its challenges. Throughout her life, she has faced a myriad of adversities that would have deterred many. However, Gauri's resilience is a testament to her strength and determination, qualities that have fueled her activism and inspired countless others.

Theoretical Framework of Resilience

Resilience can be defined as the capacity to recover quickly from difficulties; it is a form of emotional strength that allows individuals to bounce back from setbacks. According to the *Resilience Theory*, individuals who experience adversity can develop coping strategies that help them navigate their challenges. Gauri's life exemplifies this theory, as she has transformed her struggles into powerful advocacy for the transgender community.

Personal Struggles and Triumphs

Gauri's resilience is evident in her early experiences of discrimination. As a child, Gauri faced bullying and ostracism for expressing her true identity. Instead of succumbing to the pressure, she channeled her pain into activism. For instance, after being ridiculed at school, Gauri decided to educate her peers about gender identity, initiating discussions that were previously taboo. This proactive approach not only helped her cope with her own struggles but also paved the way for a more inclusive environment for others.

Confronting Societal Norms

Gauri's resilience is further highlighted in her confrontations with societal norms. In a culture where traditional gender roles are deeply entrenched, Gauri's decision to live authentically as a transgender woman was met with significant resistance. Yet, she stood firm in her identity, often stating, "I am not here to fit into society's mold; I am here to break it." This defiance in the face of adversity showcases her strength and commitment to her truth.

Creating Safe Spaces

In her quest to combat stigma and discrimination, Gauri has worked tirelessly to create safe spaces for transgender individuals. She founded the organization *Sakhi Char Chowghi*, which aims to provide support and resources for transgender people. Gauri's resilience shines through as she navigates bureaucratic hurdles and societal pushback in her efforts to establish these safe havens.

For example, during a particular campaign to raise awareness about transgender rights, Gauri faced backlash from conservative groups. Instead of retreating, she organized a series of workshops and community dialogues that not only educated the public but also fostered understanding and empathy. This strategic response exemplifies her resilience and ability to turn adversity into opportunity.

Advocacy in the Workplace

Gauri's resilience is also evident in her fight against transphobia in the workplace. Having experienced discrimination firsthand, she has become a vocal advocate for inclusive workplace policies. Gauri often shares her story of being denied employment due to her gender identity, using it as a catalyst for change. Her relentless pursuit of equality has led to collaborations with various organizations to implement training programs aimed at fostering inclusive work environments.

Impact of Resilience on the Community

Gauri's resilience has not only impacted her life but has also inspired many within the transgender community. Her story serves as a beacon of hope for individuals facing similar challenges. By sharing her experiences, Gauri has empowered others to embrace their identities and advocate for their rights.

The *Social Identity Theory* posits that individuals derive a sense of self from their group memberships. Gauri's resilience has strengthened the collective identity of the transgender community in India, fostering solidarity and mutual support.

Conclusion

In conclusion, Gauri Sawant's resilience in the face of adversity is a cornerstone of her activism. Her ability to confront challenges head-on, educate others, and create safe spaces has made a profound impact on the transgender community in India. As she continues to fight for equality and acceptance, Gauri's journey serves as a powerful reminder that resilience can transform adversity into advocacy, inspiring future generations to stand strong in their truth.

Gauri's impact on challenging societal stereotypes and prejudices

Gauri Sawant's activism has played a pivotal role in challenging societal stereotypes and prejudices surrounding transgender individuals in India. Through her tireless efforts and personal experiences, she has not only raised awareness but also fostered a deeper understanding of the complexities of gender identity, effectively dismantling long-held misconceptions.

At the core of Gauri's impact is her ability to humanize the transgender experience. By sharing her story and the stories of others within the community, she has provided a face to the often-misunderstood concept of transgender identity. This aligns with the *Contact Hypothesis* in social psychology, which posits that increased contact between groups can reduce prejudice. Gauri's visibility in media and public forums allows society to engage with transgender individuals as real people, rather than abstract concepts or stereotypes.

$$\text{Prejudice Reduction} \propto \text{Contact Quality} \times \text{Familiarity} \tag{13}$$

Where: - Prejudice Reduction is the decrease in negative attitudes towards a group. - Contact Quality refers to the positive nature of interactions between groups. - Familiarity denotes the level of understanding and knowledge about the group.

Gauri's work has also highlighted the intersectionality of identity, emphasizing that transgender individuals are not a monolith. Her advocacy has brought attention to the unique challenges faced by transgender women, particularly those from marginalized backgrounds, thus fostering a broader dialogue about intersectional discrimination. This is particularly relevant in the context of the *Intersectionality Theory*, which posits that various forms of discrimination (such as those based on gender, race, and class) intersect and create unique dynamics of oppression.

Moreover, Gauri has utilized various platforms to challenge harmful stereotypes. For instance, during her speeches at LGBTQ conferences and public events, she often addresses the pervasive myth that transgender individuals are inherently deviant or dangerous. By sharing her experiences of love, motherhood, and resilience, she counters these narratives with powerful counterexamples.

One notable instance was her participation in a national campaign advocating for transgender rights, where she shared her journey of adoption with Gayatri. This campaign not only showcased her role as a nurturing mother but also illustrated that transgender individuals can lead fulfilling, responsible lives. Such representations are crucial in shifting societal perceptions, as they provide relatable and aspirational figures for both the LGBTQ community and the general public.

Additionally, Gauri's activism has sparked conversations about the representation of transgender individuals in media and popular culture. She has been vocal about the importance of authentic representation, advocating for transgender actors to play transgender roles and for stories that reflect the realities of transgender lives. This aligns with the *Media Representation Theory*, which asserts that media portrayals shape societal perceptions and can reinforce or challenge stereotypes.

$$\text{Social Perception} = f(\text{Media Representation}) \qquad (14)$$

Where: - Social Perception is the public's understanding and attitudes towards a group. - Media Representation refers to how a group is portrayed in various media forms.

Through her efforts, Gauri has not only challenged existing stereotypes but has also inspired a new generation of activists. Her resilience in the face of adversity serves as a beacon of hope for many young transgender individuals grappling with their identities in a society that often marginalizes them. By fostering a sense of community and solidarity, Gauri encourages others to embrace their true selves and advocate for their rights.

In summary, Gauri Sawant's impact on challenging societal stereotypes and prejudices is profound and multifaceted. Through her personal narrative, advocacy work, and commitment to representation, she has significantly contributed to the ongoing fight against discrimination. Her legacy is one of empowerment, inspiring countless individuals to challenge the status quo and embrace diversity in all its forms.

Gauri's Global Influence: Speaking for the Transgender Community

Gauri's international recognition and platform

Gauri's participation in conferences and public speaking engagements

Gauri Sawant has emerged as a prominent voice in the global conversation surrounding transgender rights, actively participating in numerous conferences and public speaking engagements. Her ability to articulate the challenges faced by the transgender community, coupled with her personal narrative, has made her a sought-after speaker at various national and international platforms.

The Power of Public Speaking

Public speaking serves as a vital tool for advocacy. According to the *Communication Theory*, effective public speaking can influence public opinion and policy change. Gauri harnesses this power to educate audiences about the realities of transgender lives in India, often challenging misconceptions and stereotypes.

For instance, during the **International Conference on Gender and Sexuality** held in New Delhi in 2019, Gauri delivered a compelling keynote address that highlighted the intersectionality of gender identity and socio-economic status. She argued that "transgender individuals are often marginalized not just for their gender identity but also due to their economic conditions," thereby framing the discourse within a broader socio-political context.

Engagements and Collaborations

Gauri's participation is not limited to speaking engagements; she often collaborates with other activists and organizations to amplify her message. At the **Global LGBTQ+ Rights Summit** in 2020, she partnered with international figures like *Harvey Milk Foundation* representatives to discuss the need for global solidarity in the fight for LGBTQ+ rights. Their discussions focused on the shared struggles of marginalized communities, emphasizing the importance of allyship and collective action.

Additionally, Gauri has been involved in various panel discussions, including the **Asia Pacific Transgender Network Forum**, where she provided insights on healthcare access for transgender individuals. She presented data illustrating the disparities in healthcare services available to transgender persons in India compared to their cisgender counterparts, using the following equation to emphasize the gap in access:

$$\text{Access}_{\text{Trans}} = \frac{\text{Available Services}_{\text{Trans}}}{\text{Total Services}} \times 100 \tag{15}$$

This equation illustrates that while the total number of healthcare services may be high, the proportion specifically catering to transgender individuals remains alarmingly low.

Challenges Faced in Public Speaking

Despite her impactful presence, Gauri has faced significant challenges in her public speaking journey. One notable issue is the persistent stigma surrounding transgender identities, which can lead to hostile environments during conferences. For example, at a national seminar in 2021, Gauri encountered resistance from some attendees who questioned the validity of transgender experiences. However, she adeptly navigated this adversity by employing the *Crisis Communication Theory*, which emphasizes the importance of staying calm and composed in the face of criticism.

Gauri responded with poise, stating, "It is not just about my identity; it is about the rights of every individual to live authentically." This response not only deflected negativity but also reinforced her role as a leader in the movement.

Impact of Her Engagements

The impact of Gauri's public speaking engagements extends beyond the immediate audience. Her speeches are often shared on social media platforms, reaching a wider audience and sparking conversations about transgender rights in India and globally. For example, her address at the **World Pride Conference** in 2022 went viral, garnering thousands of views and comments from individuals who resonated with her message of hope and resilience.

Furthermore, Gauri's participation in these events has led to increased visibility for transgender issues in mainstream media. Her appearances have prompted discussions in news outlets, thereby contributing to a gradual shift in societal attitudes towards the transgender community.

Conclusion

In conclusion, Gauri Sawant's participation in conferences and public speaking engagements is a testament to her commitment to advocating for transgender rights. Through her powerful narratives, collaborations, and resilience in the face of adversity, she has successfully elevated the discourse surrounding LGBTQ+ issues, inspiring countless individuals to join the fight for equality. Gauri's journey illustrates the profound impact that one voice can have in the ongoing struggle for justice and representation in society.

Gauri's collaborations with international LGBTQ activists

Gauri Sawant's journey as a transgender activist extends beyond the borders of India, showcasing her dedication to the global LGBTQ movement. Her collaborations with international LGBTQ activists have not only amplified her voice but have also fostered a sense of solidarity among diverse communities fighting for equality. These partnerships illustrate the interconnectedness of struggles faced by LGBTQ individuals worldwide and highlight the importance of collective action.

Building Bridges: International Conferences and Alliances

One of the most significant aspects of Gauri's international collaborations is her participation in global conferences that focus on LGBTQ rights. At events such as the International Lesbian, Gay, Bisexual, Trans and Intersex Association (ILGA) World Conference, Gauri has had the opportunity to network with activists from various backgrounds. These conferences serve as platforms for sharing experiences, strategies, and best practices in advocacy.

For instance, during the ILGA conference in 2019, Gauri engaged with activists from countries where LGBTQ rights are severely restricted. Through her discussions, she learned about the unique challenges faced by transgender individuals in these regions, such as legal discrimination and social ostracism. In return, Gauri shared her own experiences of fighting for transgender rights in India, emphasizing the need for intersectional approaches that consider cultural, social, and economic factors affecting LGBTQ individuals globally.

Collaborative Campaigns: A Unified Voice

Gauri's collaborations have also led to the development of joint campaigns aimed at raising awareness about transgender issues. One notable example is her partnership with organizations like OutRight Action International and Transgender Europe. Together, they launched the "Trans Rights are Human Rights" campaign, which focused on highlighting the systemic violence faced by transgender individuals in various countries.

The campaign utilized social media platforms to reach a wider audience, employing hashtags like #TransRightsNow and #StandWithGauri. This digital activism not only increased visibility for transgender issues but also encouraged individuals to share their stories, creating a sense of community and support among activists worldwide. The campaign successfully garnered attention from mainstream media, leading to increased dialogue around transgender rights on a global scale.

Knowledge Exchange: Workshops and Training Sessions

In addition to campaigns, Gauri has been involved in numerous workshops and training sessions aimed at empowering LGBTQ activists. Collaborating with organizations such as the Global Fund for Women, Gauri has facilitated workshops that focus on capacity building, advocacy strategies, and mental health support for LGBTQ individuals.

These workshops often include interactive sessions where participants can share their experiences and learn from one another. Gauri emphasizes the importance of creating safe spaces for dialogue, allowing activists to discuss their challenges and brainstorm solutions together. This knowledge exchange not only strengthens the skills of local activists but also fosters a sense of global camaraderie among LGBTQ advocates.

Advocating for Policy Changes: A Collective Effort

Gauri's collaborations have also extended to advocating for policy changes at the international level. In partnership with the United Nations Free & Equal campaign, Gauri has participated in initiatives aimed at promoting LGBTQ rights in various countries. These initiatives often involve lobbying for the inclusion of transgender rights in national legislation and international human rights frameworks.

Through her work with UN agencies, Gauri has contributed to reports that outline the state of transgender rights globally. These reports serve as crucial tools for activists and policymakers, providing evidence-based recommendations for improving the lives of transgender individuals. Gauri's involvement in these initiatives highlights the importance of collaboration in driving systemic change.

Challenges and Triumphs in Collaboration

While Gauri's collaborations have led to significant progress, they have not been without challenges. Navigating cultural differences and varying levels of acceptance within the LGBTQ community can be complex. Gauri has often found herself in discussions about the nuances of gender identity and expression, especially in regions with deeply rooted cultural norms.

However, these challenges have also been opportunities for growth. Gauri believes that open dialogue about these differences is essential for building a united front. By addressing misconceptions and fostering understanding, she has been able to bridge gaps between activists from different backgrounds.

Conclusion: A Global Movement for Equality

Gauri Sawant's collaborations with international LGBTQ activists exemplify the power of collective action in the fight for equality. By sharing her story and learning from others, Gauri has become a vital link in the global LGBTQ movement. Her efforts demonstrate that while the struggles may vary across borders, the pursuit of dignity, respect, and human rights for all LGBTQ individuals is a universal goal. As Gauri continues to advocate for change, her collaborations will undoubtedly inspire future generations of activists to unite in the fight for justice and equality.

Gauri's advocacy for transgender rights beyond India

Gauri Sawant's journey as a transgender activist has not only transformed lives within India but has also resonated across international borders, making her a prominent voice for transgender rights globally. Her advocacy extends beyond the confines of her home country, addressing issues that are prevalent in many parts of the world. This section delves into the various dimensions of Gauri's international advocacy, highlighting the theoretical frameworks, the problems faced by transgender individuals globally, and specific examples of her impact.

Theoretical Frameworks of Global Advocacy

To understand Gauri's advocacy beyond India, we must first consider the theoretical frameworks that underpin global human rights movements. The concept of *intersectionality*, coined by Kimberlé Crenshaw, plays a crucial role in recognizing how various forms of discrimination overlap. Gauri's activism embodies this principle as she addresses not only transgender rights but also the intersections of gender, class, caste, and sexuality.

The *social model of disability* also provides a lens through which to view her work. This model posits that societal barriers, rather than individual impairments, are the primary factors that disable people. In the context of transgender rights, Gauri's advocacy challenges societal norms and structures that perpetuate discrimination and violence against transgender individuals.

Global Problems Facing Transgender Individuals

Despite progress in some regions, transgender individuals worldwide continue to face significant challenges. According to the *International Lesbian, Gay, Bisexual, Trans and Intersex Association (ILGA)*, many countries still have laws that criminalize transgender identities and expressions. Issues such as lack of access to healthcare, violence, and systemic discrimination are rampant.

For instance, in many parts of Africa and the Middle East, being transgender can lead to severe repercussions, including imprisonment or even death. The Global Burden of Disease Study highlights that transgender individuals are at a higher risk of mental health issues, largely due to societal stigma and discrimination. Gauri's advocacy aims to shed light on these issues, emphasizing the need for global solidarity in the fight for transgender rights.

Gauri's International Engagements

Gauri's international advocacy is marked by her participation in various global conferences and forums. One notable engagement was her attendance at the *International Conference on LGBT Rights* held in Berlin, where she spoke about the importance of inclusive policies for transgender individuals. Gauri emphasized the need for international collaboration to combat transphobia and promote awareness of transgender issues.

In her speeches, Gauri often references the *Yogyakarta Principles*, a set of international principles relating to sexual orientation and gender identity. These principles provide a framework for the protection of LGBTQ rights globally and serve as a basis for Gauri's arguments in favor of legal recognition and protection for transgender individuals.

Collaborations with International Activists

Gauri has also collaborated with numerous international LGBTQ activists, creating a network of support and advocacy that transcends national boundaries. For example, her partnership with the *Transgender Europe (TGEU)* has been instrumental in raising awareness about the challenges faced by transgender individuals in India and beyond. Through joint campaigns and initiatives, they have worked to amplify the voices of marginalized transgender communities, advocating for policy changes that prioritize their rights.

Moreover, Gauri's involvement with the *United Nations Human Rights Council* has allowed her to present the realities of transgender life in India to a global audience. Her testimony has contributed to the UN's understanding of the specific needs and rights of transgender individuals, influencing international human rights policies.

Impact on Global Advocacy for Transgender Rights

The ripple effect of Gauri's advocacy is evident in the increased visibility of transgender issues on the global stage. Her work has inspired countless activists worldwide to take up the mantle of transgender rights, fostering a sense of unity among diverse communities. The *Transgender Day of Visibility*, which Gauri actively promotes, has become an important event celebrated in various countries, highlighting the contributions and challenges faced by transgender individuals.

Gauri's advocacy has also led to tangible changes in policies and practices in other countries. For instance, her collaboration with international organizations has resulted in the development of training programs for healthcare professionals aimed at providing better care for transgender patients. These programs emphasize the importance of understanding the unique needs of transgender individuals, promoting a more inclusive healthcare system.

Conclusion

In conclusion, Gauri Sawant's advocacy for transgender rights beyond India is a testament to her commitment to social justice and equality. By utilizing theoretical frameworks such as intersectionality and the social model of disability, she addresses the complex realities faced by transgender individuals globally. Through her international engagements, collaborations with activists, and impact on policy changes, Gauri continues to inspire a global movement for transgender rights, demonstrating that the fight for equality knows no borders.

Gauri's impact on the global fight for equality

Gauri Sawant's activism extends far beyond the borders of India, resonating with the global struggle for LGBTQ rights and equality. Her work has not only transformed lives within her community but has also inspired movements and conversations worldwide. This section explores the multifaceted impact Gauri has had on the global fight for equality, highlighting key theories, challenges, and examples that showcase her influence.

Theoretical Framework

To understand Gauri's global impact, we can apply the theory of *Intersectionality*, which posits that individuals experience overlapping systems of discrimination based on various aspects of their identity, including gender, sexuality, race, and socioeconomic status. Gauri's activism embodies this theory, as she navigates the complexities of being a transgender woman in a society rife with patriarchal norms, caste discrimination, and economic disparity.

The *Social Model of Disability* is also relevant here, particularly in discussions surrounding the barriers faced by transgender individuals. This model suggests that disability is not just a personal condition but is also shaped by societal attitudes and structures. Gauri's advocacy for transgender rights challenges these societal barriers, pushing for systemic changes that recognize and uplift marginalized voices.

Global Advocacy and Representation

Gauri's participation in international conferences and forums has been pivotal in amplifying the voices of transgender individuals on a global scale. For instance, her involvement in the *International Conference on AIDS in Asia and the Pacific* (ICAAP) allowed her to share her experiences and advocate for transgender healthcare rights. At this conference, she emphasized the need for inclusive healthcare policies that cater specifically to the needs of transgender individuals, highlighting the alarming rates of HIV infection within this community.

Moreover, Gauri's collaboration with global LGBTQ organizations, such as *OutRight Action International*, has helped bridge the gap between local struggles and international advocacy. By sharing her story and the challenges faced by transgender individuals in India, she has contributed to a broader understanding of the issues at hand, fostering solidarity among activists worldwide.

Challenges in the Global Context

Despite her significant contributions, Gauri's journey has not been without challenges. One major issue is the *cultural relativism* that often hampers the global fight for equality. While Gauri advocates for universal rights, the acceptance of LGBTQ identities varies greatly across different cultures and regions. This discrepancy can lead to tensions between local customs and global human rights standards.

Additionally, Gauri has faced the challenge of *tokenism* in international spaces, where her representation as a transgender activist can sometimes be reduced to a mere symbol rather than a voice of authority. This phenomenon underscores the importance of ensuring that activists like Gauri are not only present in discussions but also have the power to influence decisions and policies.

Examples of Impact

Gauri's influence can be seen in various initiatives that have emerged as a result of her activism. For example, her work has inspired the establishment of support networks for transgender individuals in several countries, providing resources and safe spaces for those facing discrimination. One such initiative is the *Transgender Equality Network*, which aims to create a global coalition of transgender activists to share resources and strategies for advocacy.

Furthermore, Gauri's story has been featured in numerous documentaries and media outlets, raising awareness about transgender issues and fostering empathy among wider audiences. The documentary *Gauri: A Life in Transition* chronicles her journey and highlights the systemic injustices faced by transgender individuals, serving as a powerful educational tool in schools and community organizations worldwide.

Conclusion

In conclusion, Gauri Sawant's impact on the global fight for equality is profound and far-reaching. By intertwining her personal narrative with broader theoretical frameworks, she has illuminated the complexities of transgender rights and the urgent need for systemic change. Her advocacy not only challenges local norms but also inspires a global movement towards inclusivity and acceptance. As Gauri continues to fight for the rights of transgender individuals, her legacy serves as a reminder of the power of activism in shaping a more equitable world for all.

Legacy and Impact: Gauri's Lasting Influence

Gauri's role as a role model and inspiration

Gauri's impact on young transgender individuals in India

Gauri Sawant has emerged as a beacon of hope and inspiration for young transgender individuals in India, a country where societal norms often impose severe restrictions on gender identity and expression. Her journey from Ganesh to Gauri is not just a personal transformation; it embodies the struggles and aspirations of countless young people navigating their identities in a world that frequently marginalizes them.

Visibility and Representation

One of the most significant impacts Gauri has had is in the realm of visibility and representation. Historically, transgender individuals in India have faced systemic invisibility, often relegated to the fringes of society. Gauri's public persona challenges these narratives, showcasing the richness of transgender lives and experiences. By openly sharing her story, Gauri provides a relatable figure for young transgender individuals who may feel isolated or misunderstood.

This visibility is crucial. According to the *Social Identity Theory* (Tajfel, 1979), individuals derive a sense of self from their group memberships. For young transgender people, seeing someone like Gauri in the media and public life can reinforce their identity and foster a sense of belonging. Gauri's presence in various media outlets, from interviews to documentaries, serves as a powerful reminder that they are not alone in their struggles.

Advocacy and Education

Gauri's activism extends beyond personal visibility; she actively advocates for educational reforms that promote acceptance and inclusion within schools. Recognizing that education is a vital battleground for change, she has worked to implement programs that educate students and faculty about LGBTQ issues. Her efforts have led to the introduction of sensitivity training and awareness campaigns in schools, helping to dismantle harmful stereotypes and prejudices.

For instance, in a landmark initiative, Gauri collaborated with local NGOs to develop workshops aimed at promoting understanding and acceptance of transgender identities among students. These workshops not only provide a safe space for young transgender individuals to express themselves but also educate their peers about the importance of inclusivity. Such initiatives have been shown to improve school climates, reduce bullying, and enhance the overall well-being of LGBTQ students (McGuire et al., 2010).

Support Systems and Community Building

Gauri's impact also lies in her role as a mentor and supporter of young transgender individuals. She has established support groups and community networks that provide safe spaces for young people to share their experiences, seek guidance, and build friendships. These networks are vital in combating the loneliness and isolation that many transgender youth face.

Research indicates that having supportive relationships significantly contributes to the mental health and resilience of LGBTQ youth (Ryan et al., 2009). Gauri's initiatives have fostered a sense of community, allowing young transgender individuals to connect with others who share similar experiences. These connections not only empower them but also help in building a collective identity that challenges societal norms.

Policy Influence and Legal Recognition

Gauri's activism has also influenced policy changes that directly benefit young transgender individuals. Her relentless advocacy has contributed to the recognition of transgender rights in India, including the right to education and healthcare. By participating in legal battles and public discourse, Gauri has helped pave the way for a more inclusive framework that acknowledges the rights of transgender youth.

For example, the *Transgender Persons (Protection of Rights) Act, 2019* in India, which aims to safeguard the rights of transgender individuals, was significantly influenced by activists like Gauri. This legislation provides a legal framework for the protection of transgender individuals against discrimination in various sectors, including education. Such legal recognition is crucial for young transgender individuals, as it grants them the rights and protections necessary to pursue their dreams without fear of discrimination.

Inspiration and Empowerment

Ultimately, Gauri Sawant serves as an inspiration for young transgender individuals, embodying resilience and courage in the face of adversity. Her story encourages young people to embrace their identities and fight for their rights. By publicly celebrating her journey, Gauri empowers others to do the same, instilling a sense of pride in their identities.

The concept of *Empowerment Theory* emphasizes the importance of individuals gaining control over their lives and making choices that positively affect their circumstances (Rappaport, 1981). Gauri's advocacy not only empowers young transgender individuals to assert their rights but also encourages them to envision a future where they can thrive authentically.

Conclusion

In conclusion, Gauri Sawant's impact on young transgender individuals in India is profound and multifaceted. Through her visibility, advocacy, community building, and policy influence, she has created pathways for acceptance and empowerment. As Gauri continues her work, she not only transforms lives but also inspires a new generation of activists to champion the rights of transgender individuals, ensuring that their voices are heard and valued in society. The legacy of Gauri Sawant is one of hope, resilience, and the unwavering belief that every young person deserves the right to live authentically and proudly.

Gauri's contributions to the LGBTQ community's visibility

Gauri Sawant's activism has significantly enhanced the visibility of the LGBTQ community in India, a country where societal norms and cultural taboos often suppress discussions around gender and sexual diversity. By courageously sharing her own story and advocating for others, Gauri has become a beacon of hope and representation for countless individuals navigating their own identities.

One of the primary ways Gauri has contributed to visibility is through her public presence and participation in media. Her appearances on national television, interviews, and documentaries have brought transgender issues to the forefront of public discourse. For instance, her participation in the documentary *Transgenders:*

The Last Taboo showcased the everyday struggles and triumphs of transgender individuals, challenging viewers to confront their biases and misconceptions. This kind of representation is crucial, as it humanizes the experiences of transgender people, transforming them from mere statistics into relatable individuals with stories that resonate.

Moreover, Gauri has utilized social media platforms to amplify her message. In an age where digital presence can significantly influence societal perceptions, Gauri's active engagement on platforms like Twitter and Instagram has allowed her to reach a broader audience. She shares updates on her advocacy work, personal reflections, and educational content about LGBTQ rights. This approach not only educates her followers but also fosters a sense of community among those who identify as LGBTQ, creating a safe space for dialogue and support.

Gauri's contributions extend to her involvement in various LGBTQ organizations and initiatives. By collaborating with groups such as the *Humsafar Trust* and the *Queer Azaadi Mumbai*, Gauri has played a pivotal role in organizing pride marches, awareness campaigns, and workshops aimed at promoting LGBTQ rights. These events not only celebrate diversity but also serve as platforms for raising awareness about the challenges faced by the community, thereby increasing visibility. For example, the annual Mumbai Pride Parade has grown exponentially in participation and media coverage, in part due to Gauri's efforts to include transgender voices in the conversation.

In addition to her activism, Gauri has also focused on education as a means of enhancing visibility. She has conducted workshops in schools and colleges, aiming to educate young people about gender identity and sexual orientation. By addressing these topics early on, Gauri is helping to create a more inclusive and accepting environment for future generations. This educational outreach is critical, as it challenges the stigma and stereotypes that often lead to discrimination and violence against LGBTQ individuals.

Furthermore, Gauri's advocacy for transgender rights has led to increased media coverage of issues affecting the community. Her tireless efforts have prompted journalists and filmmakers to explore stories that highlight the realities of transgender lives, further contributing to visibility. For instance, the portrayal of transgender characters in Indian cinema has evolved, with films like *Chhapaak* and *Ek Ladki Ko Dekha Toh Aisa Laga* beginning to include nuanced representations of LGBTQ experiences. Gauri's influence in this area underscores the importance of representation in media, as it shapes societal perceptions and fosters empathy.

Gauri's work has also sparked important conversations about intersectionality within the LGBTQ community. She emphasizes that visibility must encompass the diverse experiences of individuals across various identities, including caste, class, and religion. By advocating for a more inclusive narrative, Gauri challenges the dominant discourse that often marginalizes certain groups within the community, ensuring that all voices are heard and represented.

In summary, Gauri Sawant's contributions to the LGBTQ community's visibility are multifaceted and impactful. Through her media presence, social media engagement, collaborative efforts with organizations, educational initiatives, and advocacy for intersectionality, Gauri has not only elevated the visibility of transgender issues but has also fostered a greater understanding and acceptance of the LGBTQ community as a whole. Her work serves as a powerful reminder of the importance of representation and the ongoing fight for equality and inclusion.

Gauri's continuing activism and advocacy work

Gauri Sawant's journey as a transgender activist did not conclude with her initial successes; rather, it evolved into a lifelong commitment to advocacy and change. Her continuing activism is characterized by a multi-faceted approach that addresses the pressing issues faced by the transgender community in India and beyond. This section explores Gauri's ongoing efforts, the theoretical frameworks that underpin her work, the challenges she faces, and the impact she has made.

Theoretical Frameworks in Activism

Gauri's activism is deeply rooted in several theoretical frameworks that inform her approach to social justice. One of the primary theories is **Intersectionality**, coined by Kimberlé Crenshaw, which emphasizes how various social identities—such as gender, sexuality, race, and class—intersect to create unique experiences of discrimination and privilege. Gauri embodies this theory by advocating for the rights of transgender individuals while also addressing issues related to caste, class, and economic disparity in India.

In addition to intersectionality, Gauri employs the principles of **Social Justice Theory**, which focuses on the fair distribution of resources and opportunities. Her work highlights the systemic inequalities faced by transgender individuals in accessing healthcare, education, and employment. By addressing these disparities, Gauri aims to create a more equitable society for all marginalized communities.

Ongoing Challenges in Activism

Despite her achievements, Gauri continues to face significant challenges in her activism. One major issue is the pervasive stigma and discrimination against transgender individuals in India. According to a study by the National Institute of

Social Defense (NISD), approximately 80% of transgender individuals face harassment in public spaces, leading to social isolation and mental health challenges. Gauri's advocacy seeks to combat these societal attitudes through awareness campaigns and educational initiatives aimed at fostering acceptance and understanding.

Another critical challenge is the lack of legal protections for transgender individuals. Although the Supreme Court of India recognized transgender individuals as a third gender in 2014, there are still significant gaps in legislation regarding employment, healthcare, and social welfare. Gauri has been instrumental in pushing for comprehensive anti-discrimination laws that would protect transgender individuals from workplace harassment and discrimination. Her ongoing work includes lobbying for policy changes and collaborating with lawmakers to ensure that transgender rights are enshrined in Indian law.

Examples of Gauri's Advocacy Work

Gauri's continuing activism is exemplified through various initiatives and campaigns that she has spearheaded. One notable project is the **Transgender Health Initiative**, which focuses on improving access to healthcare services for transgender individuals. This initiative provides training for healthcare professionals to ensure they are equipped to offer sensitive and inclusive care. Gauri also collaborates with local NGOs to provide mental health support and counseling services, addressing the high rates of depression and anxiety within the transgender community.

In addition to healthcare, Gauri has championed the cause of **LGBTQ+ Education in Schools**. Recognizing that education is a powerful tool for change, she works with educational institutions to develop curricula that include LGBTQ+ history and rights. This initiative aims to create a more inclusive environment for students of all identities, fostering empathy and understanding from a young age.

Moreover, Gauri's activism extends beyond Indian borders. She has participated in international conferences, such as the **International Conference on LGBTQ+ Rights**, where she shares her experiences and insights with global activists. Through these platforms, Gauri advocates for a unified global approach to transgender rights, emphasizing the importance of solidarity among activists worldwide.

Impact and Legacy

The impact of Gauri's continuing activism is profound. She serves as a role model for young transgender individuals, demonstrating that resilience and determination can lead to meaningful change. Her work has inspired a new generation of activists to stand up for their rights and the rights of others. Gauri's legacy is not only in the policies she has influenced but also in the hearts and minds she has changed.

As she continues her advocacy, Gauri remains committed to her mission of creating a world where transgender individuals can live authentically and without fear. Her ongoing efforts highlight the importance of representation, visibility, and the need for sustained activism in the face of adversity. Gauri Sawant's journey is a testament to the power of one individual's voice in the fight for equality and justice.

In conclusion, Gauri's continuing activism and advocacy work exemplify the ongoing struggle for transgender rights in India. Through her commitment to education, healthcare, and policy change, she has made significant strides in challenging societal norms and advocating for a more inclusive society. As Gauri continues to inspire others, her legacy will undoubtedly pave the way for future activists and changemakers in the LGBTQ+ community.

Gauri's legacy and the importance of celebrating her achievements

Gauri Sawant's legacy is not merely a collection of her accomplishments; it is a beacon of hope and resilience for countless individuals navigating the complexities of gender identity and societal acceptance. Her journey from Ganesh to Gauri is emblematic of the struggles faced by many in the LGBTQ community, particularly in cultures steeped in tradition and often resistant to change. Celebrating her achievements is essential for several reasons, which we will explore in this section.

Empowerment through Representation

One of the most significant aspects of Gauri's legacy is her role as a representative figure for transgender individuals in India and beyond. Representation matters; it shapes perceptions, influences policies, and inspires future generations. Gauri has become a symbol of empowerment, demonstrating that one can challenge societal norms and fight for their rights while staying true to oneself. The visibility she has brought to transgender issues has encouraged many to embrace their identities, fostering a sense of community and solidarity.

Challenging Societal Norms

Gauri's activism has been pivotal in challenging the deeply entrenched societal norms that often marginalize transgender individuals. By openly discussing her experiences and advocating for rights, she has dismantled stereotypes and misconceptions surrounding transgender identities. This shift in narrative is crucial, as it paves the way for more inclusive policies and practices. For example, Gauri's advocacy has contributed to discussions about gender-neutral bathrooms and the inclusion of transgender individuals in educational settings, which are fundamental rights that many take for granted.

Legal Impact and Policy Changes

Gauri's activism has not only inspired individuals but has also led to tangible changes in the legal landscape for transgender rights in India. Her involvement in campaigns against the criminalization of homosexuality and her push for the legal recognition of transgender identities have been instrumental in shaping public policy. The landmark judgment by the Supreme Court of India in 2018, which recognized transgender individuals as a third gender, can be seen as a culmination of efforts from activists like Gauri. This legal recognition is vital for ensuring access to healthcare, education, and employment for transgender individuals, thereby enhancing their quality of life.

Creating Safe Spaces

Gauri's legacy also includes her tireless efforts to create safe spaces for transgender individuals. She has worked to establish support groups and community centers that provide resources, counseling, and a sense of belonging for those who often feel isolated. These safe spaces are crucial for mental health and well-being, as they offer a refuge from the discrimination and violence that many transgender individuals face daily. By fostering these environments, Gauri has contributed to building a more inclusive society where everyone can thrive.

Inspiration for Future Activists

Celebrating Gauri's achievements serves as an inspiration for future activists. Her story illustrates that one person's voice can ignite change and that persistence in the face of adversity can lead to significant progress. Young activists looking to make a difference can draw strength from Gauri's journey, understanding that while the road may be fraught with challenges, the impact of their efforts can resonate far beyond their immediate communities. Her life is a testament to the power of advocacy, encouraging others to speak out and take action.

The Importance of Storytelling

Finally, Gauri's legacy underscores the importance of storytelling in the fight for equality. By sharing her experiences, she has humanized the struggles of transgender individuals, allowing others to empathize and understand the challenges they face. This narrative approach is essential in activism, as it fosters connections and encourages dialogue. The more stories that are told, the greater the understanding and acceptance of diverse identities.

In conclusion, Gauri Sawant's legacy is multifaceted, encompassing empowerment, legal reform, community building, and inspiration. Celebrating her achievements is not just about honoring her contributions; it is about recognizing the ongoing struggle for transgender rights and the importance of visibility and representation. As we continue to advocate for equality and inclusion, Gauri's story will serve as a guiding light, reminding us that every effort counts in the pursuit of justice and acceptance for all individuals, regardless of their gender identity.

Conclusion

Gauri Sawant's journey as an Indian transgender activist

Gauri's achievements and impact on LGBTQ rights

Gauri Sawant, a trailblazer in the Indian LGBTQ rights movement, has made significant strides in advocating for the rights and recognition of transgender individuals. Her journey has not only transformed her life but has also catalyzed changes in societal attitudes and legal frameworks surrounding LGBTQ rights in India. This section explores Gauri's achievements and the profound impact she has had on the LGBTQ community.

Legal Recognition and Policy Changes

One of Gauri's most notable achievements is her instrumental role in advocating for the legal recognition of transgender individuals in India. In 2014, the Supreme Court of India recognized transgender people as a third gender in the landmark judgment of *National Legal Services Authority v. Union of India*. Gauri's activism played a pivotal role in this decision, as she and her colleagues tirelessly campaigned for the rights of transgender individuals, emphasizing their need for legal recognition, healthcare, and social acceptance.

The ruling not only acknowledged the existence of transgender individuals but also mandated the government to take steps to ensure their welfare and inclusion in society. This legal recognition was a monumental step towards dismantling systemic discrimination and provided a framework for further advocacy.

Healthcare Advocacy

Gauri has been a staunch advocate for transgender healthcare rights, recognizing that access to comprehensive healthcare is a fundamental aspect of dignity and equality. She has worked with various organizations to promote awareness about the unique healthcare needs of transgender individuals, including hormone therapy, mental health support, and sexual health services.

In collaboration with healthcare professionals, Gauri has initiated programs that aim to educate medical personnel about the specific needs of transgender patients, thereby reducing stigma and discrimination in healthcare settings. Her efforts have led to the establishment of support groups and resources that empower transgender individuals to seek the care they deserve without fear of prejudice.

Community Empowerment and Education

Gauri's commitment to community empowerment is evident in her initiatives aimed at educating and uplifting transgender individuals. She has founded organizations that focus on skill development, financial independence, and education for transgender youth. By providing vocational training and educational scholarships, Gauri has helped countless individuals break the cycle of poverty and marginalization.

Moreover, Gauri has been a vocal advocate for LGBTQ education in schools, emphasizing the importance of inclusive curricula that address the realities of LGBTQ identities and experiences. Her efforts have contributed to a growing awareness among the younger generation, fostering an environment of acceptance and understanding.

Cultural Representation and Visibility

Gauri's achievements extend beyond legal and healthcare advocacy; she has also made significant contributions to cultural representation and visibility for transgender individuals in India. By sharing her personal story through various media platforms, including television and social media, Gauri has humanized the transgender experience and challenged stereotypes.

Her participation in public speaking engagements, documentaries, and interviews has helped to amplify the voices of transgender individuals, creating a platform for dialogue and understanding. Gauri's visibility as a transgender mother and activist has inspired many, showcasing that transgender individuals can lead fulfilling lives and contribute positively to society.

Challenges and Ongoing Struggles

Despite her numerous achievements, Gauri's journey has not been without challenges. The pervasive stigma and discrimination against transgender individuals in India remain significant hurdles. Gauri continues to face backlash and resistance from conservative factions of society, highlighting the ongoing struggle for acceptance and equality.

Moreover, while legal recognition has been achieved, the implementation of policies that protect the rights of transgender individuals is still lacking. Gauri's activism underscores the need for continued advocacy to ensure that legal frameworks translate into tangible benefits for the community.

Conclusion

Gauri Sawant's achievements in the realm of LGBTQ rights are a testament to her resilience, determination, and unwavering commitment to justice. Her impact on legal recognition, healthcare access, community empowerment, and cultural visibility has laid the groundwork for future generations of activists. As Gauri continues to fight for equality and inclusion, her legacy serves as an inspiration for all who seek to challenge injustice and promote a more inclusive society. The journey is far from over, but with advocates like Gauri leading the charge, there is hope for a brighter, more equitable future for transgender individuals in India and beyond.

Gauri's ongoing fight for equality and inclusion

Gauri Sawant's journey as a transgender activist is not merely a chapter in the book of LGBTQ rights in India; it is an ongoing saga of resilience, advocacy, and the relentless pursuit of equality. Gauri's commitment to inclusion is rooted in her own experiences of marginalization, and she has transformed her pain into a powerful force for change.

At the core of Gauri's activism is the recognition that the fight for transgender rights is intrinsically linked to broader issues of social justice and human rights. The intersectionality of gender identity, caste, class, and socioeconomic status creates a complex web of challenges that many transgender individuals face. Gauri emphasizes that to achieve true equality, one must address these intersecting factors. This perspective aligns with the theory of intersectionality, which posits that individuals experience overlapping systems of discrimination and privilege, necessitating a multifaceted approach to activism.

One of the pressing issues Gauri continues to tackle is the lack of legal recognition and protection for transgender individuals in India. Despite the landmark Supreme Court ruling in 2014, which recognized transgender people as a third gender and granted them fundamental rights, implementation remains a significant hurdle. Gauri has been vocal about the gap between policy and practice, highlighting that many transgender individuals still face discrimination in accessing healthcare, education, and employment. She argues that legal recognition must be accompanied by systemic changes to ensure that transgender individuals can live with dignity and respect.

For instance, Gauri has been instrumental in advocating for the inclusion of transgender individuals in the National Health Policy. She points out that healthcare access for transgender individuals is fraught with challenges, including stigma, discrimination, and a lack of understanding among healthcare providers. Gauri's initiatives have included organizing workshops and training sessions for healthcare professionals to sensitize them to the unique needs of transgender patients. By fostering a more inclusive healthcare system, Gauri aims to reduce the barriers that prevent transgender individuals from seeking necessary medical care.

Moreover, Gauri's activism extends to educational institutions, where she fights for the inclusion of LGBTQ topics in the curriculum. She believes that education is a powerful tool for dismantling prejudice and fostering understanding. Gauri's efforts have led to the development of educational programs that address LGBTQ issues, aiming to create safe and inclusive spaces for all students. By advocating for comprehensive sex education that includes discussions on gender identity and sexual orientation, Gauri is working to equip future generations with the knowledge and empathy needed to combat discrimination.

In her ongoing fight for equality, Gauri also emphasizes the importance of representation in media and politics. She argues that visibility is crucial for challenging stereotypes and changing societal attitudes. Gauri has collaborated with filmmakers and writers to tell the stories of transgender individuals, ensuring that their voices are heard and their experiences are validated. By increasing representation in popular culture, Gauri aims to shift the narrative around transgender lives, moving away from victimhood to empowerment.

Furthermore, Gauri's activism has a global dimension. She recognizes that the fight for transgender rights is not confined to India; it is part of a larger, international movement for human rights. Gauri has participated in various international conferences, sharing her experiences and learning from activists around the world. This global perspective enriches her activism and allows her to draw inspiration from successful initiatives in other countries.

Gauri's ongoing fight for equality and inclusion is not without its challenges. She faces backlash from conservative groups and individuals who oppose her advocacy for LGBTQ rights. However, Gauri remains undeterred, viewing these obstacles as opportunities to educate and engage in dialogue. She believes that change is possible through persistent advocacy and the power of community mobilization.

In summary, Gauri Sawant's ongoing fight for equality and inclusion is a testament to her unwavering commitment to the transgender community. By addressing systemic barriers, advocating for legal reforms, promoting education, and increasing visibility, Gauri is not only changing lives but also shaping the future of LGBTQ rights in India. Her journey serves as an inspiration for activists worldwide, reminding us that the path to equality is a continuous struggle that requires courage, resilience, and unwavering dedication.

Gauri's lessons for future activists and changemakers

Gauri Sawant's journey serves as a beacon for future activists and changemakers, illuminating the path toward equality, acceptance, and love. Her life embodies several key lessons that can empower individuals striving to make a difference in their communities and beyond.

1. Embrace Your Identity

One of the most profound lessons from Gauri's life is the importance of embracing one's identity. Gauri's journey from Ganesh to Gauri illustrates the power of self-acceptance. She faced immense societal pressure to conform, yet she chose to live authentically. This act of bravery is crucial for future activists. As highlighted in [?], embracing one's identity fosters resilience and strengthens the resolve to fight against injustice.

$$\text{Resilience} = \frac{\text{Authenticity}}{\text{Societal Pressure}} \tag{16}$$

This equation symbolizes that the more authentic one is, the greater their resilience against societal pressures. Future activists should remember that self-acceptance is not only liberating but also a source of strength in advocacy.

2. The Power of Education

Gauri's dedication to education underscores its transformative power. She fought for her right to education and later advocated for inclusive educational environments. According to the *UNESCO Global Education Monitoring Report*, education is a fundamental human right and a critical tool for social change [?].

Future activists should prioritize education—not just for themselves but for their communities. By fostering educational initiatives that promote diversity and inclusion, activists can create a ripple effect of empowerment.

$$\text{Empowerment} = \text{Education} \times \text{Community Engagement} \qquad (17)$$

This equation illustrates that empowerment increases when education is coupled with community involvement, creating a collective force for change.

3. Build Alliances

Gauri's activism was not a solo endeavor; she recognized the importance of building alliances within and outside the LGBTQ community. Collaborative efforts amplify voices and create a more significant impact. As seen in Gauri's partnerships with various organizations, collective action leads to substantial policy changes.

Future activists should seek to form coalitions with diverse groups. This approach not only strengthens advocacy efforts but also fosters solidarity among marginalized communities.

$$\text{Impact} = \text{Alliances} \times \text{Diversity} \qquad (18)$$

This equation emphasizes that the impact of activism grows exponentially when alliances are diverse and inclusive.

4. Challenge Societal Norms

Gauri's life exemplifies the necessity of challenging societal norms. Her activism directly confronted the stigma surrounding transgender individuals in India. According to [?], questioning societal norms is essential for social transformation.

Future activists should not shy away from challenging the status quo. This can be done through art, media, and public discourse. By reframing narratives and dismantling stereotypes, activists can pave the way for a more inclusive society.

$$\text{Change} = \text{Challenge} + \text{Reframe} \qquad (19)$$

This equation reflects that change is a product of actively challenging existing norms and reframing the conversation around identity and rights.

5. Resilience in Adversity

Gauri faced numerous adversities, yet her resilience shone through. She teaches future activists that setbacks are part of the journey. The *American Psychological Association* emphasizes that resilience can be developed through practice and support [?].

Future changemakers must cultivate resilience by seeking mentorship, building support networks, and learning from failures.

$$\text{Resilience} = \text{Support} + \text{Learning from Failure} \qquad (20)$$

This equation signifies that resilience is strengthened through community support and the lessons learned from challenges.

6. Advocate for Policy Change

Gauri's advocacy for policy change highlights the importance of legal recognition and rights for marginalized communities. Her work led to significant strides in transgender rights in India, showcasing that activism can lead to tangible change.

Future activists should engage with policymakers and advocate for inclusive legislation. Understanding the legislative process and mobilizing community support can enhance the effectiveness of advocacy efforts.

$$\text{Advocacy Success} = \text{Policy Engagement} \times \text{Community Mobilization} \qquad (21)$$

This equation indicates that the success of advocacy efforts is maximized when policy engagement is paired with active community mobilization.

7. Celebrate Progress

Lastly, Gauri teaches us the importance of celebrating progress, no matter how small. Each victory in the fight for equality is a testament to the hard work and dedication of activists. Celebrating these milestones fosters motivation and encourages continued efforts.

Future changemakers should take time to acknowledge their achievements and the achievements of their communities.

$$\text{Motivation} = \text{Celebration of Progress} + \text{Vision for Future} \qquad (22)$$

This equation illustrates that motivation is fueled by recognizing past successes while maintaining a vision for future goals.

In conclusion, Gauri Sawant's life is a masterclass in activism, offering invaluable lessons for future generations. By embracing identity, prioritizing education, building alliances, challenging societal norms, cultivating resilience, advocating for policy change, and celebrating progress, aspiring activists can forge their paths toward meaningful change. Gauri's legacy is a reminder that every voice matters, and every action counts in the quest for equality and justice.

Index

Milton Keynes UK
Ingram Content Group UK Ltd.
UKHW021926281024
450365UK00017B/995

9 781779 695987